KENT R. HUNTER

The Jesus Enterprise

Engaging Culture to Reach the Unchurched

Abingdon Press
Nashville

THE JESUS ENTERPRISE
ENGAGING CULTURE TO REACH THE UNCHURCHED

Library of Congress Cataloging-in-Publication Data

Hunter, Kent R., 1947-
 The Jesus enterprise : engaging culture to reach the unchurched / Kent R. Hunter.
  p. cm.
 Includes bibliographical references and index.
 ISBN 0-687-00647-3 (binding: adhesive : pbk. : alk. paper)
 1. Church growth. 2. Christianity and culture. 3. Church growth—United States.
4. Christianity and culture—United States. I. Title.
BV652.25.H855 2004
266—dc22
2003026663

04 05 06 07 08 09 10 11 12 13—10 9 8 7 6 5 4 3 2 1

MANUFACTURED IN THE UNITED STATES OF AMERICA

*To all enterprising Christians who engage
the culture for Jesus Christ*

CONTENTS

FOREWORD

Kent has engaged my mind and heart! He has gone to the heart of how to relevantly and realistically communicate the gospel in today's world. The purpose of this work is to help all of us who are serious about being Christ followers to do a better job in identifying and meeting the felt needs of our culture. By doing this we will be able to bond with people and build bridging ministries that truly engage people in the community around us so that their lives will be transformed.

What was so helpful to me in this book were the numerous examples and illustrations of how enterprising mission centers are so effectively and creatively engaging their culture for the sake of the gospel.

My encouragement for you as you read this book is to ask God to prayerfully open your mind and heart to what enterprising epicenters are possible in your own community.

Prayer is always the prelude to opening the floodgates of faith and fruitfulness. Now as you faithfully follow Jesus and humbly serve his flock may you, "Be on guard. Stand true to what you believe. Be courageous. Be strong. And everything you do must be done with love" (1 Corinthians 16:13-14).

Walt Kallestad
Senior Pastor
Community Church of Joy
Glendale, Arizona

ACKNOWLEDGMENTS

With every enterprising project, including the production of a resource like this, teamwork is an important part of the equation. God has blessed me with a great team of people, and I'm grateful for their input on various levels.

In the production of this book, I'm especially thankful for the work of Kelly Hahn. He edited and revised the manuscript several times, making it the most valuable use of time for the reader.

I'm also grateful for David Price, who has worked with me on church architectural consultations and who has supplied some examples of church buildings for this book. Thanks also to my friend and associate church consultant Bruce Barber for the special help with this project.

I feel especially blessed by those people with whom I have worked on a regular basis: Cheryl Kroemer, Shelly Hinkley, Pam Sheppard, Olive Hinkley, Neil Bachman, Frank Grepke, Barry Kolb, Bob Whitesel, Cindy Warren, and Autumn Brown, as well as many others who support the ministry in various ways. I'm also thankful for colleagues in ministry including Jon and Peggy Campbell, Walt Kallestad, Tim Wright, Paul Sorenson, and Chip MacGregor. I'm thankful for those who read the manuscript and provided valuable input: Rob Olson, Julie Carmicheal, and Dave and Holly Langwell. Thanks to those who are special partners for Church Doctor Ministries: Robert Shaw, Bob and Kari Grimm, Barbara Grimm, and Mike and Nancy Friend. Special thanks to my board of directors and friends: Jim Manthei, Wayne Register, Roger Miller, Jerry Boyers, Greg Ulmer, and Rob Olson.

As always, I appreciate my family, who also are a part of the sacrifice that goes into a project like this: My wife, Janet, our son, Jon, and our daughter, Laura.

INTRODUCTION

Bob and Marsha grew up in a typical Protestant church in the Midwest United States. They met in school, were married, and pursued their careers. They went to church, as had their parents and grandparents. And, as their parents and grandparents had, they were raising their children in the church.

One day they heard a missionary speak during the Sunday service, and God planted a seed—a call—for them to become "foreign missionaries." They felt God's urging to spread the gospel to somewhere far away where the people were quite different. So they started taking classes at a local Bible college. The program was offered to "second career" people—those who already had a job but could take classes part-time and gain a deeper understanding of the Bible and the history of the church. They were able to complete a few of the courses through the Internet. After several years, both Bob and Marsha received a degree, which enabled them to connect with a parachurch organization. This ministry provided the platform to send missionaries all over the world. They declared their intention and were accepted. A few months later, they received a call to serve God in northwest Thailand.

Before they went, Bob and Marsha were required to attend classes at a mission school. It was their last stop before they traveled overseas. At this mission school they received special training. They began to learn the basics of the language. They learned the different customs and beliefs held by the people they would be reaching. But beyond the skills and education they received, the most important lessons they encountered occurred deep within themselves. In the process of training, their understanding of cultures was transformed. They experienced a monumental paradigm shift. They would never be the same.

After finishing mission school, Bob, Marsha, and their two children made the long and exciting journey to their assigned village in northwest Thailand. They were sent to evangelize an unreached group—people who had never been exposed to Christianity. When they arrived at the village, they began the relatively long and tedious process of connecting with the people in the village. They began developing relationships. As their language skills developed, they engaged people in conversation. They discovered there were several divine signals within the environment of the group. These signals pointed to a singular felt need. First, there was a large percentage of the people who had some form of dysentery. Second, it seemed there was no defined place that could be called a village toilet. Third, the runoff of the frequent rains collected in small pools where people would obtain their fresh water. These signals pointed toward a genuine felt need: the need for a clean, fresh water supply.

While Bob and Marsha had been trained to preach the gospel of Jesus Christ and build a church, they had also been trained, first and foremost, that they needed to engage the culture. They wanted to demonstrate the integrity of their faith in a loving and caring Lord. They also needed to penetrate the relationship barrier that naturally exists between people God wants to reach and those trying to reach them. Bob and Marsha never thought to enter that village and start by building a church building with a sign in front inviting anyone who wanted to come. They understood that to engage the culture, they would (1) meet a need (2) that would show genuine care (3) and provide a conduit for conversation (4) as well as build relationships that would be the platform for them to speak in a relevant way about new life in Jesus Christ. Their first missionary strategy was to help the people get clean water. They had learned how to engage the culture.

Every once in a while, Bob and Marsha would think back to what ministry had been like in their local church. Whereas before they had welcomed any non-Christians who happened to show up at church, here, they were engaging the culture by meeting the need for fresh, clean water. The difference in the level of engagement was immeasurable!

Janet is a preschool teacher at her church. When asked why she serves in that capacity, she reflects that it is her ministry. She says, "Many of the parents who bring children to this preschool aren't Christians. They aren't driven here by the motive of exposing their children to Jesus Christ. Most of them want quality education for their children before they enter kindergarten. It's a test drive for our Christian elementary school, which has a strong reputation in the community." Then Janet went on to explain, "Even though some may not have religious motives, the preschool gives me an opportunity to interact with those parents. Once their children start counting numbers and saying the alphabet, those parents feel good about what we do. That provides me an opportunity for a relationship with influence. About that time, the children start asking at home, 'Why don't *we* pray before meals? We do at school!'"

Through her ministry to preschoolers, Janet finds divine opportunities through conversations with their parents. She can share what Jesus Christ has meant to her and invites them to the congregation's contemporary, visitor-friendly worship service. Many times, these parents accept her invitation, and when they do, Janet meets them, sits with them, and offers to hold their children. While building a foundation in the lives of children in their formative years, God gives windows of opportunities for relevant, personal mission outreach.

How do you react to this?

A magazine featured a short article titled "The *New* New Thing." "Churches around the country are seeking new ways to attract followers. The Family Christian Center in Munster, Indiana, has opened a Starbucks in the lobby of the nondenominational church to create a more inviting atmosphere. The Brentwood Baptist Church in Houston is set to open a

McDonald's. And in Wells, Maine, the Messiah Christian Church has an on-site fitness center."[1]

Your reaction to what you just read will depend on your *posture* as a Christian. That posture defines your behavior. Your behavior has an influential effect on the people in your network of relationships. Your posture—as it is expressed in the community of believers (the church)—has enormous implications on your church's influence on your community and world. As George Hunter has explained in his book *Radical Outreach*, "In this new secular mission field, local churches are called to be missionary congregations. The local church's main business has shifted from chaplaincy to apostolicity. . . . In any mission field, including ours, the people of God are called and sent to be *in* the world—as salt and light, in ministry and witness—but not to be *of* the world."[2]

Our work at Church Doctor Ministries with thousands of churches reflects that many Christians, and their respective churches, have taken postures toward the culture around them that is not in concert with the biblical message (www.churchdoctor.org). Even worse, their postures are contradictory and counterproductive and contribute to the dwindling influence of Christianity. That negative effect is seen not only in the erosion of Christian influence in the West (particularly North America) but also wherever the church has once flourished, only to slip into a post-Christian status.

Many floundering churches are made up of well-meaning Christians who are nice people, love the Lord, and are going to heaven. However, they are ineffective for the mission of God to their own neighbors. Without knowing it, they hurt the cause of Christ in this world. Some have forgotten what it means to have a missionary posture, but most have never learned. Tom Bandy calls this missionary posture "The Christian Way." He says that, "The Christian Way is not alienated from the world, but leads into the world. It cares so much for the world as to be in conversation with it."[3]

When you walk into Community Christian Church in Naperville, Illinois, you are greeted by surroundings that proclaim a message. Unlike many church facilities, you don't find yourself in a spacious lobby or church office. Instead, you are standing in the Ground Level Café, a coffee and espresso bar that's not simply a twenty-first-century version of the "fellowship hour" (www.communitychristian.org/whoweare/inthenews.htm). It operates seven days a week and is a frequent hangout for the young, upwardly mobile people who live nearby. Many of those people come from unchurched backgrounds.

In the perception of unchurched people, most church buildings look like a fortress with a moat around it. So what is the Ground Level Café? It's a bridge! Tim Wright, in his excellent book *The Prodigal Hugging Church*, says, "The kingdom of God is radically different from culture. But the ruler of that kingdom became radically like culture in order to embrace it. The Incarnation clearly demonstrates that God approaches culture by permeating the secular with the sacred and the sacred with the secular. Unfortunately, we in the Church tend to build walls to separate the two."[4]

Community Christian Church is using the Ground Level Café as a bridge to bring the sacred to the secular and the secular to the sacred. They are engaging the culture. It is what Jesus did. It is, in biblical form, what I refer to as the *Jesus Enterprise*. It underscores the reality that Christianity, like electricity, flows best where there is good contact.[5]

As we work with a wide variety of Christian churches, we see a common thread among those who are effectively reaching people for Christ. They reach out to the community in the same way Father Simeon did in a story I heard told by Dale Galloway, Dean of the Beeson International Center for Biblical Preaching and Church Leadership at Asbury Theological Seminary in Wilmore, Kentucky (www.ats.wilmore.ky.us).

Father Simeon was a Catholic priest who felt the need to minister to those with leprosy. So, he boarded a ship and sailed to a Hawaiian island, where the lepers were kept. When he got off the ship, a leper reached out to him with a hand that was covered with leprosy. Father Simeon instinctively drew away from the hand and the disease thought to be caught by touching. Word spread rapidly through the colony that Father Simeon would not take the hand. So, they would have nothing to do with him or his Jesus.

When he got to the neglected church, all he saw was rubble and ruin. He rang the bell for Sunday service, but no one came. They didn't want anything to do with the man who wouldn't touch them. Days and weeks went by with Father Simeon getting more discouraged. When the next ship came in, he went down to the dock to get on board and go back home. But, as he looked around the dock, he saw a load of lumber and realized they really needed that lumber in the colony. He told the captain to drop off the lumber. The captain refused and said the load was to go to the next island. Again, Father Simeon told the captain to drop off the lumber. And, again, the captain said no. Father Simeon was now caught up in a cause that was greater than himself. He walked over to a little girl on the ship who was to be dropped off at the leper colony, picked her up, walked over to the captain, and told him that if he didn't drop off the lumber, he would touch him with the little girl. The captain put the lumber on the dock. Again, word spread through the colony about Father Simeon, but this time it was about his showing love to the the little girl by touching her. When he got back to the colony, they all gathered around him. He had won their hearts when he had lost himself to the cause.

He announced to them that they weren't going to build a church first. They were going to build a hospital because that was the greatest need among the people of the island. Father Simeon learned to engage the culture of the people he was trying to reach. His ability to reach them not only included a physical reach, but a posture—a mental attitude—that he could be successful only when he lost himself in his cause, overcame his fears, was willing to take a risk, and focused on meeting a felt need. Why is this so difficult? Jesus said, "whoever wants to save his own life will lose it; but whoever loses his life for me and for the gospel will save it" (Matthew 16:25).

For most people, intentionally engaging the culture around them requires a major paradigm shift. It includes a different way of looking at yourself, your church, your community, and your world. This book is intended to create a paradigm shift in your Christian posture and your approach to the culture around you. It is intended to challenge you to consider Jesus' ministry as an enterprise.

Enterprising ministry is an effort intentionally designed to engage people around you. It requires an ability to abandon the structural aspects of your faith that seem comfortable to you but are foreign to non-Christians. While the gospel itself sometimes offends people, the way you share the gospel should not.

While the truths of Christianity never change, the packaging must change continually in order to meet the demands of an ever-changing world and culture. Although many Christians don't recognize this, packaging can make all the difference. Years ago, a cannery in LeSueur, Minnesota, was faced with a financial struggle. Since sales were continually short of their expectations, a product analysis was ordered. The report said the company's vegetables were as good or better than anything else on the market—they didn't need to be changed. Instead, the little known company changed the shape of its cans, which gained better visibility on the supermarket shelves. Sales began to increase. They didn't change what was inside, just how it was presented on the outside.[6] They didn't change the substance of their product. They engaged people who were the target for that product. That made all the difference.

There is no "problem" with the content of the Christian message. There is nothing about the good news of Jesus Christ that is irrelevant for the twenty-first century. The issue is the packaging used by those who share the "product" with others. This book is about engaging non-Christians around you and building bridges so the gospel can do what the gospel does: change people's lives. This is a book about sharing that good news in such a way that you are not a roadblock, but a bridge. It is doing ministry the way Jesus did. This is the heart of the Jesus Enterprise.

This book will focus on the creation, use, and dangers of enterprise ministries. It includes more than two hundred models of enterprise ministries. They are provided not as "canned programs" that you should replicate in your church, but as models to inspire strategies for engaging people in your own community from the strength and uniqueness of your own congregation.

This book provides a holistic view of ministry that engages the culture in a way that connects deeds of Christian charity with strategic elements for evangelistic opportunities. Further, it will direct you toward the goal of discipleship as it is reflected in the Great Commission.

The tone and posture of this book is to provide transformation for your local congregation as you are engaged in the community so that you can develop a mission mentality through stimulated missionary thinking and approaches to ministry. Enterprise models are provided descriptively but also carry a prescriptive orientation to energize you and other leaders in your congregation toward creative and strategic thinking that engages people for the sake of the gospel. This book will identify not only the financial benefits but also the abuses to avoid as you join the Jesus enterprise.

CHAPTER ONE

WHAT'S YOUR POSTURE?

For the last two thousand years, the Christian Church has seemingly had a love/hate relationship with culture.   Tim Wright

W hen I was in high school, I experienced a growth spurt. It affected my posture to the point that I needed to wear a back brace. It was necessary because poor posture affects all the other systems in the human body. If left uncorrected, it would have caused many serious problems.

Proper posture also affects the Body of Christ. Every Christian has a posture to the culture around them. Your posture is reflected in your attitudes and beliefs regarding culture. The level of your effectiveness in God's kingdom work depends greatly on your posture. A healthy posture allows God to accomplish God's purposes in and through you. An incorrect posture creates difficult, and sometimes painful, problems.

Discussions on Christianity and culture aren't new. In 1951, theologian H. Richard Niebuhr wrote the book *Christ and Culture*. In it, he describes the various approaches Christians have taken concerning the place of Christ in connection with culture. The chapters discuss Christ *against* culture, the Christ *of* culture, Christ *above* culture, Christ and culture *in paradox*, and Christ *as transformer of* culture.[1] But while Niebuhr's work wrestled with the position of Christ and culture, this book is written to help you, as a Christian, relate to culture as Jesus did for the purpose of mission. *Jesus engaged the culture around him.* He had to. It was a part of his mission, and he's given you a part in that mission as well.

Walt Kallestad, senior pastor of Community Church of Joy in Glendale, Arizona says, "The church exists for no other reason than to participate in God's mission. *Without mission there is no church.*" Kallestad believes this is the

> time for the people of God to become a radically *inclusive* community.... all are invited to sit at God's table. There are no outsiders for Jesus. All are included, all are invited.
>
> Ironically, the only folks in the Gospels who could be called outsiders are those who, out of religious pride and prejudice, *exclude themselves* from God's inclusive reign.[2]

This "all inclusiveness" is a posture toward people outside the Body of Christ. It is an intentional positioning toward the culture that is inviting and engaging. When you are involved in efforts that engage the culture, you are part of an enterprise ministry. Enterprise ministry meets real needs. Loving and caring for people without other motives is the genuine integrity of Christianity. Yet, as it meets needs, enterprise ministry builds bridges that engage people. This engagement ultimately provides a platform for relevant gospel communication. Why? You share the good news in the context of a relationship that began when you met someone's real needs. There are other ways to do it, but the gospel makes more sense when it's shared by someone you know, rather than two strangers knocking on your door or a person with a shaved head and a strange outfit handing out tracts at an airport.

Tim Wright describes it this way:

> For the last two thousand years, the Christian Church has seemingly had a love/hate relationship with culture. On the one hand, we know that Jesus invites us as his followers to go into culture and make disciples of all peoples. He calls us to be in the world in order to share his life-transforming love with others.
>
> On the other hand, as people transformed by the love of Christ, we want to align ourselves with his values and increasingly distance ourselves from the impact of the negative values of culture. Although Jesus calls us into the world, the apostle Paul warns us not to conform to culture—or not to be of the world.[3]

Wright asserts that Christians often focus more on not being *of the world* than they do on being *in the world*. When this happens, Christians tend to withdraw from culture and create their own subculture. In this subculture, they preserve their style of music, dress, structure, liturgy—everything that makes them comfortably insulated from the world and its culture. The problem arises when non-Christians attend events, usually worship services, within this subculture. To the non-Christian, much of it seems "foreign." The language is strange, the buildings are odd, the music is radically different, and the symbols make no sense. These are communication barriers. The components of this subculture work against Christians who want to share the good news of Jesus with people far from God, which is exactly what God has called us to do!

Tackling this issue is crucial because Christians often forget *why* the church exists. In the Christian subculture, the church exists for the members. But the church that Jesus envisioned and commissioned exists for others. My friend Charles Van Engen points out that the Bible "doesn't say, in John 3:16, that God so loved *the church* that He gave His only begotten Son. It says that God so loved *the world* that He gave His only begotten Son. Our mission is the world, not the church."[4] Walt Kallestad also adds, "At the opening ceremony for Disney World, Walt Disney, the creative genius behind the theme park, proclaimed, 'We didn't build this for ourselves. We built it for others.' "[5] Jesus' Great Commission calls us to have the same attitude.

Five Postures

As I work assessing and consulting churches, I often see symptoms of poor posture. Without correction, these symptoms hinder the very purpose of the local congregation. In other words, the effectiveness of God's work comes down to people like you—and the posture you have toward your culture.

Throughout history, Christians have chosen one of five different postures toward culture. Four of these postures have a *debilitating* effect on the Christian movement: retreating from culture, ignoring culture, judging culture, and preserving culture. The rest of this chapter will examine those four postures. The fifth one allows God to affect other people in a profound way (which will be the focus of the next chapter). Unfortunately, this correct posture is frequently lost in the lives of Christians and the work of churches—the very places where it should thrive! As we look at these various postures toward culture, I challenge you to evaluate your own posture with an open and receptive heart.

Retreating from Culture

There are many examples throughout history where Christians have chosen to retreat from culture. I live in northeast Indiana, a region that is home for numerous Amish communities. The Amish are wonderful, hardworking, and simple people who, by religious conviction, retreat from modern culture. The Amish believe they have chosen a period in history when life was better and, supposedly, more "Christian." Frozen in time, they resist various forms of modernism.

This isn't God's plan for the Christian church. The message of Christianity isn't confined to one specific period of time.

Christianity transcends time and culture, even though today's culture may not be "as Christian" as the one the Amish picked.

Jesus spent most of his public ministry under the scrutiny of the religious leaders. They were so steeped in old customs and traditions that they were unwilling or unable to see that God was fulfilling his promise of a Messiah, even though Jesus was right in front of them! In their retreat from the culture, they were unable to receive the good news Jesus had for them. He compared them to old wineskins into which he was trying to pour new wine (Matthew 9:17).

The extreme case of Christian retreat from culture is life in convents and monasteries. Some live in complete isolation from the rest of the world, growing deeper in their walk with Christ. It is possible that God is calling some to that life. But the majority of Christians are commissioned to reach out to others who have yet to meet Christ. Salvation carries with it the challenge to engage others.

Many Christians have retreated to their own version of convents and monasteries. What would you do, for example, if your son or daughter brought home a friend who was gay? How would you react if a friend brought a prostitute to your Bible class? When you see a part of your culture that makes you uncomfortable, do you tend to back away from it? Is your faith integrated into all of life? Or do you tend to separate the sacred from the secular and retreat from culture? Ask yourself, "Is that what Jesus did? Is that what he called his church to do? Is that his plan for his mission through you in this world, to retreat from culture?" Retreating from culture doesn't address issues; it just prevents you from bringing Christ's influence to the solution.

Ignoring Culture

Throughout history, Christians have often assumed the posture of ignoring the culture. I remember attending a church only two Sundays after the September 11, 2001, attack by terrorists on the United States. We were only twelve days removed from the haunting images of the twin towers. We were gripped by fear. The nation was still reeling, but God, in grace and mercy, was drawing people to worship. Spiritual receptivity was soaring, and people far from God were coming face-to-face with their own mortality. Some people were coming back to church. But in the worship service I attended, the pastor's sermon seemed to ignore what was going on in the world. Although he preached a wonderful exposition from a portion of Acts, he never once engaged the concerns and questions that every single attendee had that morning. He delivered a sound, theological message, but he ignored the culture.

Evidence of Christians ignoring culture is strong. In this twenty-first century, major ethical issues concerning genetic research, cloning, and biotechnology are making headlines on a regular basis. But most Christians are curiously silent on the issues. It's almost as if they don't like the difficult challenges that such issues raise. They ignore them in hopes that they'll eventually go away. Of course, that's wishful thinking—they never will.

In his challenging book, *Learning the Language of Babylon,* Terry Crist talks about the church's distance from political structures. "The Church is allowed a great deal of freedom, but at the same time expected to stay in her place. So we find ourselves seated at the table of unilateral disarmament, saying to the enemy, 'Just give us our tax-free status, leave us alone, and we will leave the popular culture to you.'"[6] Christians sometimes ignore culture. This is why, for many years, churches in the U.S. allowed blatant segregation of African Americans and, before that, their enslavement. Crist also points out that one of the dangers of ignoring culture, especially in the twenty-first century, is that the "Church may continue to retreat to the cultural sidelines and revert to an expression of Christianity that prides itself in irrelevance."[7]

I see this in some of the churches I serve as a consultant. An elderly greeter will smile and say, "Good morning," with a twinkle in his eye to guests and members as they enter the building—at least until a teenager with a nose ring and tattoos walks in. He pretends he doesn't even see him. Or the building committee that refuses to install a baby-changing table in the bathroom, even though many of the people moving into the new subdivision are young parents. Or the elder who changes the words on the church's sign, using archaic language: "Thou believest the prophets?" In each case, they're ignoring the reality of the world in which they live.

It is easy to ignore problems that create discomfort, embarrassment, or fear of confrontation. Many people refuse to talk about the HIV virus. It's hard to imagine why; so many millions are sick and dying from this terrible condition. Dr. Doug Kinne left his successful medical practice to serve in the area of medical missions. With his wife, Jan, Doug trained health care workers from numerous countries all over the world. Before he died, Doug wrote a course on how to serve people with the HIV virus. Today, that course is training medical missionaries all over the world on how to go into areas of great need and effectively serve people stricken with HIV. Through the context of their loving mission work, each missionary has incredible opportunities to demonstrate God's love and to share the good news of Jesus Christ. But work like that would never have happened if Doug had lived a posture that ignored culture.

What is your posture? Remember the story Jesus told the religious leaders about the man who was beaten up and robbed on the road between Jerusalem and Jericho (Luke 10:30-35)? Two people passed him by and ignored his plight, not wanting to get involved. They were religious people who were ignoring the obvious need of a bleeding and broken person. Many Christians read that and think, "Well, I'd never do that!" Yet Christians fail just as monumentally when they ignore a broken and bleeding culture because it is uncomfortable to engage it. What about you?

Judging Culture

None of these postures are self-contained. You can ignore culture and retreat from it as well. You can have one or both postures and also judge the culture. Judging culture occurs when individuals act as judge, jury, and executioner of the culture around them. It is the most overtly antagonistic posture toward culture.

Have you ever wondered why unchurched people often refer to Christians as hypocrites? Interview unchurched people and you will discover something startling: Christians bring this criticism upon themselves. It isn't that Christians shouldn't ever disagree with the culture. If they never had a word about culture that pointed out the wrongs, Christians would be in the posture of ignoring culture. The real issue is that, in the absence of anything positive, many Christians take the posture of being totally negative. The world knows clearly what Christians are against, but it's not too sure what they're for. When non-Christians hear the pronouncements of judging Christians, they make the connection that Christians think they're perfect, or at least better. Then, when unbelievers see these imperfect Christians fail, they conclude they are hypocrites. This makes it nearly impossible for judging Christians to have any kind of evangelistic influence. As Ravi Zacharias pointed out: "The old Indian proverb holds true: Once you've cut off a person's nose, there's no point giving him a rose to smell."[8]

How do you avoid ignoring culture without judging it? A proactive change in positioning can make a noticeable difference. You could be against abortion, but that has a negative ring to it. It makes unbelievers think you're positioning yourself in a posture of judgment. Instead, you could be pro-life, which is a positive approach to the same issue. Likewise, you could be against sexually offensive material and adult nightclubs, or you could be for healthy families and purity.

This posture of judgment doesn't just show up in individual Christians. Unfortunately, many sermons emphasize what's wrong with certain types of people. You can even hear messages that focus on what's wrong with other *Christians*. This is what occupies the void when proper biblical truths aren't upheld. Even denominations have this problem. Most denominations have a biannual or triannual national denominational meeting. It's about the only time the media covers the organizational side of the Christian church in the press. What most often makes the news? Usually, it's the rampant division and infighting in the denomination. It's no wonder many unbelievers hold the perspective that Christians have a posture of judgment. What about you? Do you talk about what you're against more than what you're for? Are you guilty of a judgmental posture?

Preserving Culture

One of the most challenging issues that faces the church and Christians is what Terry Crist calls our own "*cultural* captivity."[9] If you're a Christian who lives for others, then your own stylistic preferences within Christianity will be subordinated to reaching others. But if you are postured for yourself, then you will want to, at all costs, preserve the culture that is familiar to you. Throughout history, many well-meaning Christians have carried the gospel to different cultures and people around the world. However, as they did, some superimposed their own cultural baggage on others. Many Western missionaries required primitive people to wear Western clothes, speak the missionaries' language, eat the missionaries' food, live in places built like the missionaries' dwelling back home, and worship in styles that are not a part of the local culture. These are extreme forms of cultural chauvinism. They are the opposite of what the apostle Paul said when he proclaimed, with a missionary mind-set, "I become all things to all people, that I may save some of them by whatever means are possible" (1 Corinthians 9:22b).

But many Christians perpetuate the subculture of the church where they were raised. They have favorite songs from their childhood. Those songs were the favorite songs of their parents and their grandparents. They became foundational aspects of their Christian subculture. Some pillars of this subculture include musical styles, building structures, church furniture (like pews), favorite Bible translations, hymnbooks, and dress codes. The problem is that the culture is dynamic. It is constantly changing. When non-Christians are subjected to a preserved culture from another time or another tradition, as mentioned before, it makes the gospel appear irrelevant, old, out-of-date.

In the New Testament, a young evangelist by the name of Stephen was stoned to death (Acts 6–8). At first, it would appear that Stephen was stoned to death by non-Jewish unbelievers because he was preaching the gospel of Jesus Christ. But that wasn't the case. Stephen died because the religious leaders accused him of speaking against the customs and the Temple. It was the threat to the traditions—and the building—that upset them. Stephen was challenging the perpetuation of their subculture. It upset them so greatly, they riled up the crowd to the point where they brutally killed him.

Perpetuating and preserving your own style of Christianity (not the content!) indicates confusion between the core truths of Christianity and the way it is packaged. What is your posture? Have you ever caught yourself saying, "But we've always done it that way?"

These are the four prevalent, unbiblical postures toward culture: retreating from culture, ignoring culture, judging culture, and preserving culture. But there is one posture toward culture that will allow you to be salt and light to people without Christ. That happens when you engage the culture. It's what Jesus did, and it's the subject of the next chapter.

Enterprising Thoughts

- The level of your effectiveness in God's kingdom work depends greatly on your posture.
- The gospel makes more sense when it's shared by someone you know, rather than two strangers knocking on your door or a person with a shaved head and a strange outfit handing out tracts at an airport.
- "Our mission is the world, not the church." (Charles Van Engen)
- The effectiveness of God's work comes down to people like you.

- Salvation carries with it the challenge to engage others.
- Retreating from culture doesn't address issues; it just prevents you from bringing Christ's influence to the solution.
- Christians fail when they ignore a broken and bleeding culture because it is uncomfortable to engage it.
- The world knows clearly what Christians are against, but it's not too sure what they're for.
- "The old Indian proverb holds true: Once you've cut off a person's nose, there's no point giving him a rose to smell." (Ravi Zacharias)
- Do you talk about what you're against more than what you're for?
- If you are postured for yourself, then you will want to, at all costs, preserve the culture that is familiar to you.
- Have you ever caught yourself saying, "But we've always done it that way?"

Next Step Questions

1. How have you interpreted your relationship with culture? What new insights did you learn through this chapter?
2. Do any of the four postures discussed in this chapter describe your current position toward culture? Your church's posture?
3. If you're retreating, ignoring, judging, or preserving, what might have led you to assume that posture?
4. Spend some time meditating on John 3:16. What is God's posture toward the world? What do you think God intends for your posture to be?

CHAPTER TWO

INFLUENCING CULTURE BY ENGAGING CULTURE

Imagine how different every Christian's outreach encounters will be—in the neighborhood, in the school, in the workplace, in the world—if we take into account our divine appointment as ambassadors.   Paul Borthwick

While many Christians retreat from, ignore, judge, or preserve their own culture, Jesus engaged culture. When Jesus met the Samaritan woman at the well, he didn't retreat from her—despite the fact that he was a Jew and she was a Samaritan (John 4:5-30). He didn't ignore her, as most other Jewish men would have done (note the reaction of Jesus' disciples). He didn't pronounce judgment on her—although he

13

did speak truth in the context of their conversation. And he didn't preserve the unwritten rules regarding male/female public conversation. Instead, he was committed to interacting with her and engaging her in a conversation at the end of which he would tell her how her life could be changed forever (more on this in the next chapter).

When Jesus told the parable of the prodigal son, he spoke of several events that would have infuriated the Pharisees (Luke 15:11-32). His story strongly contradicted their views of how the people of God should respond to others. They were scandalized—offended—by what they perceived to be improper behavior. First, the father gave the inheritance to the son before the proper time. That was unheard of in that culture. Second, the son went out and squandered the money. Third, he had to make a living by taking care of pigs—the most disgusting, unclean animals imaginable among those of the Jewish culture. Fourth, when the son returned home, Jesus said the father ran to embrace him (requiring him to lift his garment). Putting this in the story condoned a hideous embarrassment in the view of the culture.

Why did Jesus tell this story this way? The "improper" actions of the father indicate that God is willing to go to the scandalous extreme to engage the culture for the salvation of people. Jesus was telling a story about himself. Jesus, and his death on a cruel cross, was God's mechanism for bringing lost people back. The parable of the prodigal son is a powerful example of the scandalous extent to which God will go to reach people—by engaging culture. In fact, in Jesus Christ, God is willing to become culture for the sake of lost people (Luke 15:11-32).

In Acts 17, the apostle Paul meets the Athenians on Mars Hill. There were statues for gods strewn everywhere. They even had a statue for the "unknown god" just so they wouldn't leave anyone out. Paul truly wanted to reach these people, and Scripture says, "While Paul was waiting in Athens for Silas and Timothy, he was greatly upset when he noticed how full of idols the city was" (Acts 17:16). It is obvious Paul had strong feelings about what he saw. But would retreating from Athens, ignoring the gods, judging the Athenians, or making them understand his culture influence them to where he could effectively share the gospel? Instead, Paul engaged the culture. He pointed to the statue for the unknown god. Instead of blasting them for their pagan idolatry, he told them who that unknown god was, the God who made all the rest. He even referenced one of their poets (Acts 17:16-34).

If you engage the culture, you have the opportunity to influence it. None of the other postures give you that privilege. In the early years of Christianity, the pagans celebrated the fertility holiday of Esterus. It happened every spring in the northern hemisphere. Life was bursting forth with new plants and leaves on trees, and animals were giving birth after the long winter season. Had the early Christians been postured to retreat from culture, they would have considered this holiday a total taboo and fled. Had they been postured to ignore culture, they would have started their own sectarian activities and let the pagans celebrate Esterus to their own damnation. If they had been postured to judge culture, the Christians would have marched and protested against the pagan holiday and, in an extreme, could have taken physical and violent action toward those who celebrated Esterus. Had they been postured to perpetuate their own culture, they would have continued in their own Christian rituals and customs. They would never have thought of engaging the *concept* of the Esterus celebration. But early Christians saw the model of God in Jesus. They saw Esterus as the celebration of new life. Even though it was determined by the phase of the moon in the spring (which was pagan in nature) and changed dates every year, they decided they would impregnate the meaning of the pagan holiday with belief in the power of the resurrection and new life in Jesus Christ. This is how the pagan holiday of Esterus was eventually overtaken by the Christian celebration we now know as Easter.

Radical changes like this continue to happen whenever people are aggressive about engaging culture. Have you ever wondered what the impact would be if the American national anthem was updated? It's nice and nostalgic, but it was written more than two hundred years ago. It doesn't fit with the singing style of many people today and, for most Americans, doesn't evoke the emotion that it could if it reflected our culture. Many performers who sing the national anthem at professional sporting events put their own spin and style to the national anthem. They are trying to engage the contemporary culture with the old form.

I once heard an elementary class say the pledge of allegiance on a radio station—in the form of rap! It was really quite inspiring! The point is this: Saying the pledge of allegiance in a way that allowed them to be relevant to their own culture had an enormous impact on the kids and the meaning of what they were saying.[1]

To what extent will you subordinate your preferences in style and tradition in order to reach your culture? To what degree will you sacrifice to distribute a message that is culturally sensitive to the people you're trying to reach? As Tim Wright has clearly pointed out,

> one of the major causes of conflict in churches today is not the issue of whether or not we should reach out to the community. Most believers admit, even if it's begrudgingly, that that's what the church is called to do.... The cause behind much of the chaos in churches and the reason why many congregations fail in their attempts at innovative mission is the practical application of mission itself... the relationship between church and culture.[2]

It's a classic problem I see in churches: The people say, "We want to reach the lost," but when that involves changing what touches them on a heart level, they say, "Oh! We didn't know it meant changing that!" Rick Warren, in his book *The Purpose-Driven Life*, describes becoming a world-class Christian. Rick says it requires a shift from self-centered thinking to other-centered thinking.[3]

Engaging the culture involves intentionally finding needs that will bring you in contact with people who are not a part of your church. Doing this allows you to work with people in ways that meet their needs and provides you with opportunities to share the love of God.

Christianity is based on authentic relationships. Walt Kallestad points out,

> The key word is *authentic*. An authentic relationship is one that does not have an ulterior motive....In our postmodern world [people] are *tired of being used* and are naturally suspicious of all relationships that seem to have hidden agendas.
>
> We want to be wanted for who we are and not just for what we do or give or bring.
>
> ...When the church becomes a place where relationships have more than instrumental value, it will be a place that people seek rather than flee.[4]

Engaging ministry does *not* mean meeting the needs of people to manipulate them into heaven. It means genuinely caring about them in their everyday needs and, in the context of spiritual concern, also caring about their eternal destiny. People respond to you when you are interested in engaging them in authentic relationships. Seeing faith in action stimulates people to want to know more about what fuels your desire to meet needs.

Perhaps you are familiar with the traditional evangelistic crusades of Billy Graham (www.billygraham.com). Those have reached people for Christ all over the world. But in Riverside, California, Pastor Greg Laurie of Harvest Christian Fellowship knew that if he were to lead a crusade, engaging his culture would require some changes (www.preachtheword.org). Over the years, more than one million people have attended annual Harvest crusades. But they aren't anything like the traditional crusades. They create a festive atmosphere with Christian rock concerts, skateboard exhibitions, and car shows. It's the best way for his church to engage people from his culture.[5]

One of the classic examples of a ministry seeking to engage culture is the ministry of Dr. Robert Schuller of the Crystal Cathedral (www.crystalcathedral.org). The *Los Angeles Times* carried an article about the telemarketing that his ministry does.

The telemarketing ministry autodials four hundred thousand homes a week, inviting people to watch Dr. Schuller's television show "Hour of Power." When Dr. Schuller was asked about "this new approach," he said, "I'm not sure the approach is new. It's just new technology." A spokesperson for Dr. Schuller said that the telemarketing approach is really doing nothing different than what Dr. Schuller himself did forty-five years earlier when he knocked on doors and invited people to church. At one time, Dr. Schuller had a worship service at a drive-in theater where people could worship in their cars. The consistent principle in Schuller's approach is his willingness and passion to engage the culture.[6] Dr. Schuller is just one of many examples of how God uses enterprise ministries to make a difference in the lives of people. Gary McIntosh says it this way: "Biblical church growth takes place in churches that are indigenous to their mission field.... Simply stated, *life-giving churches relate to their communities in culturally relevant ways.*"[7]

But as long as Christians cling to the four nonproductive postures, opportunities will be missed. Mohandas Gandhi studied in South Africa as a young man. When he tried to attend a Christian church, he was turned down because of the color of his skin. It is said that Gandhi rejected not Christ, but the perverted picture of Christ that he was given. Gandhi never became a Christian because he saw Christianity as Western—it just wasn't something he could take back home to India. *What would have happened if Gandhi had become a Christian?* Considering his incredible influence on India throughout his lifetime, hundreds of millions of people could have been converted from Hinduism and Islam to Christianity. It was a missed opportunity that underlines a crucial truth about spreading the Christian faith: How you engage culture does make a difference.

Enterprising Thoughts

- God is willing to go to the scandalous extreme to engage the culture for the salvation of people.

- If you engage the culture, you have the opportunity to influence it.
- Engaging the culture involves intentionally finding needs that will bring you in contact with people who are not a part of your church.
- Seeing faith in action stimulates people to want to know more about what fuels your desire to meet needs.
- How you engage culture does make a difference.

Next Step Questions

1. Why is a posture that engages culture critical to fulfilling the Great Commission (Matthew 28:18-20)? How is Jesus' life an example for us to follow?
2. Describe a time when you saw a person, or a church, engaging culture. It may have been through a medical service, carnival, or auto repair ministry. How did that example change your perspective on engaging culture?
3. Reread the parable of the prodigal son (Luke 15:11-32). What does it tell you about the extent to which God will go to bring people back? How does that change the way you perceive your current posture?

CHAPTER THREE

ENTERPRISING THE AUDIENCE

God is committed to developing a people who will reflect his character in this world, and his character always expresses concern and compassion for the afflicted....Whether or not we keep our eyes open determines whether or not we will grow in compassion. Expanding our hearts always starts with what we choose to see.

Bill Hybels

My first call to pastor a church was in Detroit, Michigan. The congregation was an old Anglo church located in an inner-city neighborhood of many young, African American families. Having a passion for evangelism and the fulfillment of the Great Commission, I sensed a real opportunity—most of our neighbors were unchurched. Our congregation had been declining for ten years. In fact, it had decreased in membership 67 percent in the decade prior to my arrival. There were many times that first year when I felt the church should have called a funeral director, not a pastor. But I didn't want to give up.

Though I had spent eleven years preparing for ministry (four years of college, four years of seminary, and three years acquiring a Ph.D. in theology), I quickly realized I had no awareness of how to strategically reach that community. I asked my denominational leaders if they could point me to a strategic ministry that would work in a cross-cultural situation like mine. They said they didn't know what worked but added that, if I found out, I should let them know. I ended up in the Doctor of Ministry program at Fuller Seminary in Pasadena, California. For three years, I went two weeks at a time and, after returning, implemented what I learned into my ministry. The church donated my time to go; I donated the rest. It was an incredible experience! I spent time studying in the School of World Mission, the largest such school in the world (www.fullerseminary.net). It wasn't long before I realized that, in the context of my church, I was on a mission field but was never trained to be a missionary. If I, as a pastor, didn't know how to "do mission" in my own neighborhood, how could I expect my people to know what to do?

I began to understand a form of ministry that, only now, I can identify with terminology. I was learning the seeds of enterprise ministry. It's how missionaries penetrate cultures with the gospel of Jesus Christ in a relevant way. And it worked for us in that cross-cultural outreach in Detroit.

In my studies, I learned that the first thing missionaries do is study the community. They listen. They observe. They diagnose what God is doing in the culture. I learned that in any culture, at any given time, there are real needs that people feel—called *felt needs*. The missionaries identify which of those felt needs their Christian ministry can meet. Then they work to meet those needs, develop relationships, and share the gospel. In that context, the gospel isn't foreign but relevant. How could something so simple escape the training of a person like me with a Ph.D. in theology?

So we went to the community, visited in homes, listened, and learned. It quickly became apparent that many of the young African American families had grade school aged children. One of their top priorities was strong education for their children.

They wanted their kids to get better jobs, live in better homes, and have better lifestyles. They even said they were willing to pay the price for better education. But they felt trapped in a public school system that they perceived as greatly deteriorated. There were few options available to them. Detroit public schools were bussing children across town—not for racial balance but because the schools in our neighborhood were overcrowded. Young African American mothers and fathers were complaining about their children being crammed into classrooms with one teacher and forty students. As I listened, with missionary ears and a Great Commission heart, I thought about this felt need. Then I looked at our all white church, filled with nice Christians who were beginning to see their Great Commission marching orders as a mandate to reach the new community. Some of my preaching and teaching was about to pay off!

Long before I came, in the 1950s, our church had built a huge educational wing. In fact, it had one of the largest Sunday schools in our Lutheran denomination. It boasted vacation Bible schools with thousands of children. Those days were gone. But the building remained. We began to investigate. With just a few hundred thousand dollars in renovations, it could be made into a first-rate school that would house a preschool, kindergarten, and eight grades. It already had two gymnasiums, three kitchens, and several other multipurpose rooms, few of which were used at all. What an opportunity!

With the typical risk that accompanies enterprise ministry, we renovated the building, called a number of teachers, and started a preschool through eighth grade school—all within six months! We offered our neighbors the opportunity to provide their children with quality education. They lined up at the doors and sacrificed much to get their kids into school. It wasn't a moneymaker, but we paid the bills.

The teachers we hired were trained as Lutheran school teachers. But we gave them extra training. They were required to take evangelism training and learn church growth principles. They were trained to be missionaries. Not all of them made it. Some could not see themselves as missionaries in their own country.

Within just a couple of years, this declining, old, all white congregation began to grow. Young African American families were joining the church and being assimilated into leadership positions. The church was once again reaching its community. It had become a thriving enterprise ministry.

Enterprising

In their book *Boiling Point*, George Barna and Mark Hatch identify a study by two economists, Joe Pine II and James Gilmore. These economists have identified how the economy has changed from being one related to goods and services to one related to experiences. One of the dynamics of this is that experiences, even more than goods and services, draw people and engage them. My grandparents went to the corner store in the neighborhood to get whatever that store offered. It was a limited market. My parents went to stores that included several items and more choices. As I grew up, I could go to a shopping mall. I had choices not only of goods but also of stores, all built together like a little village. In my children's generation, they find not only goods and services at that shopping mall but also an experience. That's why people "hang out" at the mall. And that's why malls provide music, food courts, arcades, and decorative environments that engage people.

According to Barna and Hatch, organizations like Disney and America Online (AOL) are successful because they sell commodities and service in the context of a desirable experience.[1] Think about it: The Hard Rock Cafe is not just a place to eat. It's an experience. This is also true for McDonald's, Starbucks, and many other restaurants and forms of sports and entertainment. It is also true of a growing number of churches! In his book *The Great Good Place*, sociologist Ray Oldenburg says that understanding and diagnosing the experience is a discipline called environmental psychology.[2]

One of my life goals was to attend a Green Bay Packers game at Lambeau Field. I'd been a Packer fan primarily because I like to watch people who do whatever they do with passion. That would be the Packers (most years) and their fans (always). One year, I was given tickets for my son, Jon, and me to attend a Packers game. We didn't go just to watch a football game; you can do that on television. We went for what TV can't give. We spent time in the parking lot at the largest tailgate party I have ever seen, both before and after the game. It was an experience!

So is good Christianity. Church, done well, is an engaging experience. It interacts with people in an engaging way. In that sense it is an enterprise. It "enters" into the lives of people. When it's done well, church is relevant because it engages the culture. I don't just mean worship, but everything the church does.

There is a popular secular radio program called "Delilah After Dark" (www.radiodelilah.com). Delilah never preaches (formally) and never talks about herself as a "Christian." But in an incredibly marvelous and sensitive way, she interacts with people by phone and plays secular music selections that have a message. She constantly talks about God and frequently directs people to prayer. In a sense, Delilah probably directs more people toward Christianity in a soft and preevangelistic way than most Christian radio stations—to which many unchurched people would not listen. Her transparency and incredible acceptance of those who phone is one of the most astounding demonstrations of grace. Her radio show, in a sense, is an enterprise ministry. The television show *Touched by an Angel* is another example (www.touched.com). While these examples are not "religious broadcasting," there is a very sensitive engagement that taps into the spiritual interests of people outside the walls of Christianity as well as those within. They are meeting felt needs.

Audience Match

In marketing, this is called matching the audience. In banking, it's called using the currency the bank accepts. In theology, it's called the Incarnation. God wanted to reach people so he showed up in Jesus Christ—in the flesh. It is the key to effective enterprise ministry. Whenever the church engages the culture in a productive way, it does so by speaking the heart language of the people it's trying to reach. If you want to reach your culture, your audience gives you important clues about how you should communicate. A remarkable example of this is the preaching of Rob Bell, Jr. at Mars Hill Bible Church in Grandville, a suburb of Grand Rapids, Michigan (www.mhbcmi.org). The way Rob engages the audience with intense Bible content is astounding. It is also effective. This growing church has taken over a shopping center to handle its ministry!

In the mid-1990s, Yale Professor of Surgery Richard Selzer wrote *Mortal Lessons: Notes on the Art of Surgery*. In this book, he tells the story of a young woman who had a malignant tumor on her cheek. When he performed the operation, it was required that he clip a nerve in order to remove the whole tumor. Doing this left her mouth distorted. The next evening he made his post-operative rounds. As he walked into the room to check on this young woman, he realized he had walked in on a moment of romantic privacy between the young woman and her husband. The surgeon was impressed as he saw them gazing at each other. He saw how they transparently loved each other. At that point, the woman looked up, saw her doctor, and said, " 'Will my mouth always be [crooked] like this?' He said, 'Yes . . . it will. It is because the nerve was cut.' " At this point, her husband remarked that it was "kind of cute" and reached down and kissed her. Selzer writes, "I [was] so close I [could] see how he twists his own lips to accommodate to hers."[3]

That story is a parable about the Incarnation. It's what it means to be an extension of Christ to the people you are called to reach. Many of those people are broken, hurt, and twisted. But the Lord of the harvest—Jesus, this enterprising God—calls you and me to begin where those people are, rather than where he would like them to be (Hebrews 2:14).

Jesus was the divine presence of God in the flesh. It is possible that he could have commuted from heaven to earth each day if he wanted. But, obviously, he chose not to do that. In his enterprising mission to reach the world, he chose to live among the people he desired to reach. He breathed our air, walked on our ground, and understood the pain of our humanity. It shows that Jesus does not reach people in a vacuum, even though he can do whatever he wants.

"The Church Doctor" radio program aired on approximately three hundred Christian radio stations across the United States, Canada, Australia, the Caribbean, and England for several years. As I travel and speak at conferences, I'm introduced as "The Church Doctor." It's interesting that even though most people have never met me personally, they feel like they know me because they've listened to my program. It's what is known as a "radio relationship." After numerous exposures, people sense they have a relationship with a person they've never met. But when we meet at a conference, that relationship takes on a whole new dynamic. It's interesting: Before, they knew me as "The Church Doctor." Now they also know me as Kent Hunter. It's an incarnation of sorts. It's a deeper level of engagement.

The Ministry of Jesus

Jesus' ministry is one story after another of engaging activity. In fact, it is this engagement with people that separates him from so many other religious leaders.

When Jesus met that Samaritan woman at a well, she was not there to attend a religious service. She was not there to get her life straightened out. She certainly didn't come there to become a missionary to her village. Her primary mission that day was to get some water—nothing more, nothing less. After her encounter (read: engagement) with Jesus, her priorities were so reordered that the text says she left her water jar as she went to talk to the people in her village. She encouraged them to come and see the man who had told her everything she had ever done. She left a changed woman.

The enterprise lesson is to look at *how* Jesus conducted ministry. The *how* is the strategy. The first clue is that he spoke with this woman. As mentioned earlier, in that culture, talking to a Samaritan woman in public was a significant risk for Jesus. It provided an opportunity for gossip, misunderstanding, rumors—it could have wrecked his ministry. So this Samaritan woman was no doubt significantly shocked when this Jewish rabbi engaged her in conversation.

In enterprising fashion, Jesus engaged her at the point where every enterprise ministry must begin: at the level of the receiver's need. He talked to her about water. He invited the cultural engagement by saying to her, "If you only knew what God gives and who it is that is asking you for a drink, you would ask him, and he would give you life-giving water" (John 4:10). By the end of the conversation, she identified Jesus as being someone significantly different. She didn't leave that encounter feeling guilty or judged. She didn't leave feeling that Jesus was utterly irrelevant. She didn't leave burdened with a religious "to do" list. She left as a person so engaged by the power of God that she rearranged her priorities for the purpose of engaging the people in her village. That immediate multiplication is typical for God's work when it's done in an enterprising way. It doesn't result in *growth* of the kingdom, it results in an *explosion*. The Christian movement is intended to be an enterprise. People who are broken, twisted, and troubled are the target of God's affection. They are like the prodigal son. In enterprising fashion, Jesus came to embrace prodigals on God's behalf.[4]

If you want to engage your culture, join the Jesus enterprise and do what Jesus did. Embrace people like the Samaritan woman. Like Jesus, you'll probably be misunderstood and criticized by religious people. But do it because that's what God's work is all about.

What Is Enterprise Ministry?

An enterprise ministry can be defined as: *identifying and meeting felt needs in the culture, genuinely caring for others, building relationship bridges, and communicating the gospel in a relevant way.* This chapter unpacks what it means to meet felt needs and build bridges. Chapter 4 will look at engaging culture for the purpose of relevant gospel communication.

Felt Needs

Any target group God provides for you to reach has felt needs of some kind. These are not needs *you* perceive these people might have. These are needs *they* genuinely feel. Sometimes these needs are symptomatic of a deeper need. That's not surprising: In the big picture, they need a relationship with their Creator. They need to be restored by the forgiveness and grace of Jesus Christ. The woman at the well had a felt need for water. She also had a need to get her marital life straightened out. But her real need was new life and a restored relationship with God. Notice that Jesus started with her felt need at the surface.

The truth is that very few people walk into a pastor's office and declare, "I'm a sinful person deeply in need of repentance, regeneration, sanctification, and connection with a Christian community where I can receive God's Word and be discipled for Jesus Christ." More likely, they don't walk into a pastor's office at all. They meet someone like you at the well of life. They meet you where you work. They are neighbors. They are students. They are friends and relatives. Their subject is not regeneration, but tension in their home life, a problem with an irritable boss, financial struggles, bad news from the doctor, concern about war, worries about a kid on drugs, and a whole range of other felt needs. As a Christian involved in enterprise ministry, you have the opportunity to be sensitive to those felt needs and recognize them as windows of opportunity. They are ways God says to you, "I am giving you an opportunity with this person to engage them, care for them, show them God's love, grow a relationship, and share good news for the sake of their eternal destiny as you meet the immediate needs they are facing."

On September 11, 2002, the first anniversary of the attack on the World Trade Center, First Christian Church of Canton, Ohio, decided to have an outdoor community worship service on some property the church had purchased for relocation (www.fcccanton.org). The preaching pastor, John Hampton, admitted afterward that he wondered how many people would show up. Thousands came. Why? When you engage culture and meet needs, people respond. On that same weekend, thousands of U.S. churches had church as usual, with no special emphasis on one of the most horrific and traumatic events inside America in history. For many churches, it was business as usual—and the usual crowd.

The opportunity to meet felt needs connects you to where people live and breathe in their cultural context. Christian Schwarz has pointed out, "it can be shown that 'pushy' manipulative methods [of evangelism] represent the exact opposite of the practice we learn from growing churches. Their secret is the way they share the gospel in a way that meets the questions and needs of non-Christians."[5]

Many of the churches that activate their people for this most successfully are those in urban areas where felt needs seem more critical and are perhaps more obvious. Maybe it's because enterprise ministry is required for the urban church if it is to survive. For example, Salem Baptist Church of Chicago is a congregation that has engaged its community in significant ways (www.sbcoc.org). Pastor James Meeks has energized the people to be heavily engaged, not just in the redemption of people but in the redemption of the community around the church. The church has literally claimed, in prayer, the blocks around the congregation and the people who live in those areas. This, like many successful urban ministries, is a church that operates in the dimension of enterprise ministry.

Landa Cope, in her excellent book *Clearly Communicating Christ*, says it this way:

> [A] dynamic aspect of [Jesus'] communication was His servant approach.
>
> At some point in history the Church forgot this. We became focused on our message rather than on serving our audience. The burning question wasn't, "Where are people hurting? How can we apply the Gospel to meet those needs?" Instead it

became, "Are we being faithful to Scripture? Is that the exact meaning of those words? Are we communicating in balance with the whole of the Bible?"

Instead of pouring our hearts into reaching people, our passion became defending the message. If God felt that way, John 3:16 would have read, "For God so loved the *message* that He sent His only Son."

Jesus didn't come to defend the message. The message of God's eternal truth is just fine, thank you. It stood before the creation of the earth, and it will stand when all heaven and earth have passed away (Matthew 24:35). It's people who are in danger! God so loved the *world*.[6]

Building Bridges

The bridges that God uses are relationships. They are divine conduits that provide the environment to not only meet felt needs with integrity but also engage the culture in a way that leads to a Christian witness.

Many Christians feel the primary strategy for effectively reaching unchurched people is to make sure the message is pure. While a clear articulation of biblical truth is essential, there are much stronger issues from the perspective of those who are unchurched. When unchurched people are asked why they are not involved in a church, they frequently talk about issues of friendliness and relevance, not biblical accuracy. John Maxwell tells of how research reported in the *Wall Street Journal* indicated that 83 percent of the people who do not return to a restaurant say they did not go back because of the service. Yet restaurants continue to think they're in the food business. They're not in the food business. They're in the people business![7]

The same could be said about the church. The word *ministry* is from the idea "to wait at tables." Sometimes churches focus only on the food (spiritual food), but people never get to the food because the service is bad. You can have the greatest teaching in the world, but if you're throwing numerous roadblocks in front of people (the service is bad), they're not going to come back to hear your great teaching. When asked why they return to a church they visited, most people respond that they did so because it was a friendly church and the worship services seemed relevant. The content *and* the environment spoke to their lives in a way that had meaning. The church engaged them. It was a good experience.

As you meet felt needs in the context of enterprise ministry, your connection—relationship—is very important. You're not manipulating someone so you have an opportunity to share the gospel. You are beginning with a genuine concern for the person and their specific challenges. As you establish contact, you start praying and looking for an opportunity, a divine window for sharing the gospel. It is important to ask God for sensitivity to what I call the "trigger." In most cases, there is a trigger event that enhances a person's receptivity to your witness of the faith. Trigger events include just about anything in a person's life that represents transition or tension. It could be losing a job, suffering bankruptcy, or inheriting a large sum of money. It could be a relocation of residence, the start of college, the birth of a child, a death in the family, retirement, the start of a new occupation, or any other transition experience.

Developing contact is key in building a relationship of integrity, particularly for postmodern generations. Postmodern people, on the front end of their spiritual journey, are not interested in knowing whether or not the Bible is true. Many postmodern, pre-Christian people tend to reject the concept of absolute truth. The postmodern view is: what's true for you may be different than what's true for me, but both, paradoxically, are considered to be true. While this is contrary to the Scripture, postmodern people will discover this only as they make progress in their spiritual journey. On the front end, they are more interested in knowing if Christianity *works*. In other words, they want to know if God makes a difference in your life.

This makes sharing the gospel much easier. You're not required to confront someone. You don't need to develop an "argument" or be able to present a "watertight case." The key is to speak from your heart and be a witness. People want to know how God has made a difference in your life. When you went through difficulty, did God make a difference? Did God help you through a health problem? A job challenge? A transition? A difficult relationship? And if so, how did you experience that help? Remember, people are after an *experience!*

Meeting felt needs and building bridges are indispensable to the Jesus enterprise. Ultimately, this leads to engaging culture for the purpose of relevant gospel communication, which is the subject of chapter 4.

Enterprising Thoughts

- In any culture, at any given time, there are real needs that people feel—called felt needs.
- Church, done well, is an engaging experience.
- To reach culture, your audience gives you important clues about how you should communicate.
- In enterprising fashion, Jesus came to embrace prodigals on God's behalf.
- An enterprise ministry can be defined as: *identifying and meeting felt needs in the culture, genuinely caring for others, building relationship bridges, and communicating the gospel in a relevant way.*
- Enterprising ministry doesn't result in *growth* of the kingdom, it results in an *explosion.*
- The truth is that very few people walk into a pastor's office and declare, "I'm a sinful person deeply in need of repentance, regeneration, sanctification, and connection with a Christian community where I can receive God's Word and be discipled for Jesus Christ."
- People want to know how God has made a difference in your life.

Next Step Questions

1. How do you approach discovering felt needs in your community? Why is it crucial to get the perspective of

people outside your church, rather than a brainstorming summary from a committee inside the church?

2. How did Jesus build bridges to the people he wanted to reach? What did his miracles and compassion communicate to people? How can that empathy and ministry be duplicated today?

3. Why are meeting felt needs and building bridges necessary *before* communicating the gospel in a relevant way?

4. Who is in your context of engagement? How can you learn about their felt needs? Develop your relationship further? Look for a trigger event? Share the good news?

CHAPTER FOUR

CULTURE-SENSITIVE COMMUNICATION

Eat what is set before you. Jesus (Luke 10:8)

As an enterprising Christian, you develop evangelistic opportunities by demonstrating acceptance. The next time you talk with an alcoholic whose life is a mess, just say to yourself those words Jesus said to the crowd, "Who wants to throw the first stone?" (John 8:7). It's called grace.

But engaging the culture also requires you to understand the language, style, and dynamics of the culture. Your interest isn't in a statistic for your denomination or church's worship services. Your focus and concern is on each person as an individual created by God, not a means to help grow your church.

In the Jesus enterprise, your goal is to introduce people to raw Christianity, not a certain brand of religious subcultural baggage connected with your religious style. Don't fall into the trap of preserving styles and expressions that are familiar to you and make you comfortable. Most non-Christians didn't grow up in that subculture, or they grew up in it and rejected it. Promoting that baggage is more of a hindrance than a help and more of a detriment than a strategic plan. Your goal is to *engage* the culture.

Terms of Engagement

Capturing the power of enterprise ministry requires adherence to the terms of engagement. These terms reflect the ministry of Jesus as well as the worldviews reflective of the New Testament church.[1] These terms of engagement redirect you as a Christian in the way you relate to others, as well as the way you serve. It can radically change and revitalize your church. There are five strategic marks of a culturally engaging church.

1. Outward Bound

While the Great Commission (Matthew 28:19-20) clearly challenges you and me to "go" to people, what usually happens is that we establish a building and then focus most of our attention on inviting people to come to us. The commission to go to people doesn't focus entirely on physical travel but includes a willingness to meet people at their level, communicate in their language, get involved in their culture, understand their ways, identify their joys, recognize their hurts, and accept them where they are, recognizing that it is God who will ultimately take them to a different level.

In your church, an outward posture means shifting from a rigid institution to recapturing what God intends for it to be: a movement. The gathering of believers isn't merely a retreat or sanctuary, it is a training ground and launching pad for God's army of believers called to penetrate the world and flavor it, just as salt flavors food (Matthew 5:13).

2. Subordinate Everything You Are

It may seem strange to suggest you should make compromises as a Christian. But as a Christian involved in enterprise ministry, that is *precisely* what God has called you to do. This is what Jesus did. He compromised comfort for mission. He compromised his position in heaven. He took on human form and became one of us. His commitment to others was so strong, he literally "emptied himself" (Philippians 2:5-11 NRSV). That doesn't mean he compromised his divine nature, but, rather, he set aside everything else because of his passion to reach lost people.

3. A Sensitivity to Needs Found in the Culture

If you are involved in enterprise ministry, you are constantly watching the news, reading the newspaper, and observing public forums as you search for hints of needs in the community.

Sensitively identifying needs requires knowing people who are not Christians and developing genuine relationships with a listening ear and a learning attitude. How many unchurched people do you know well? The sad truth is that many Christians have very few relationships with truly unchurched people. This is partly due to the inappropriate choice of postures that Christians make toward culture. Many feel that to go into a bar in order to talk to unbelievers is compromising Christian behavior, or that eating lunch with people who tell off-color jokes is somehow betraying the Christian witness.

I admire the way Bill Hybels, pastor of Willow Creek Community Church in South Barrington, Illinois, develops the crew for his sailboat. It is made up mostly of unchurched people. Bill uses this environment as a context for developing relationships with people outside the church. Their common element is the love for sailing, but Bill has an opportunity through that common denominator to develop relationships that lead to a witness for Christ. Some of his stories about crew members crossing the line of faith are powerful reminders of the importance of engagement.

In the same way, Jesus didn't retreat from, judge, or ignore people outside the religious institution. He openly engaged them in order to reach them. What was the reaction of the religious leaders of his day? They called him a drunkard and a party animal who associated with all the wrong people. Jesus was clear to point out that his purpose was to seek out and save the lost (Luke 19:10). He communicated to the religious leaders that it is sick people who needed a physician—as if anyone is perfectly well before God (Matthew 9:12)!

4. A Passion to Communicate at the Level of Heart Language

Christians tend to create barriers that keep non-Christians from becoming engaged with the faith. One of them is the persistent use of their own subcultural language. I grew up in an era when King James Version Bibles were used in our Sunday school. The subtle message to me was that the Bible was a foreign language. Still today, I visit many churches where worship songs include words like "thy" and "thou," which are not familiar to anyone today except Shakespearean scholars and subculture Christians.

The heart language of people is the language they use on the street. It is the language in which they dream. Does this mean you should do away with all traditional styles of worship? On the contrary. Many Christians raised in the church have been enculturated to religious language patterns from previous centuries. They are spiritually stimulated by King James language. It is their heart language. To reach newcomers to the faith and keep the lifelong Christians, provide two worship services—one traditional, one contemporary. Keep the content the same; vary the flavor. I call this the Baskin-Robbins approach to worship communication.[2]

After retirement, my grandparents moved to Florida, a state that has many retired people. My grandparents were Lutheran, and, as children, spoke German at home. It was still their religious heart language. I know that because at times I would travel with them, and when they went to bed, I heard them pray the Lord's Prayer together—in German. But despite all the Lutheran churches in the area, none offered German services—not even on an occasional basis. It would have been wise for one of the local churches to provide a service in German because there were many elderly people in that community from a German heritage. Their early growth in the faith occurred in that language. The failure to have German services for those older people was just as much a betrayal of this principle of heart language as a congregation that fails to provide a contemporary service for the millennial generation.

5. A Commitment to Genuine Relationships of Integrity

You may have been taught, as I was (though subtly) that Christianity is all about belonging to an institution. In fact, you may have been taught that knowing about Jesus and being able to recite Bible passages was somehow the pinnacle of Christian faith. But Christianity is all about relationships. First, it is a relationship with Jesus Christ. That is one reason Jesus shared the imagery of the Vine and the branches; it paints the picture of a close connection (John 15:1-8).

But Christianity also moves out and touches other people through relationships. Throughout history, it's the way the church has grown. The Christian faith is spread by one person who comes in contact with another. Christianity is not so much taught or promoted as it is caught by sharing, experientially, through relationships as people are infected with the reality of your relationship with Jesus Christ. Your relationship with someone far from God is the bridge over which the Holy Spirit travels the journey of the Great Commission.

Mark Conner explains the importance of relationships and what they mean for the life of the church:

God wants us to shift our focus from just having events to the development of meaningful relationships between people, so that the church becomes a caring Christian community.

For too long, church has become a thing we go to, an event or an experience, rather than a community of people networked together in loving relationships. The Church is to be much more than a crowd gathering for an event. It is to be a closely networked group of people serving Christ together. Genuine loving relationships provide the care that people need and the context in which life transformation can take place.[3]

Enterprise ministry includes an unconditional acceptance of others. This is what Jesus did. "Jesus successfully extended both arms of salvation to those who were lost, disenfranchised and without hope in Israel. Through compassionate interaction He extended the opportunity for them to receive eternal life, while also reaching out to feed the hungry, heal the sick and encourage the outcast."[4]

Relevant Gospel Communication

The ultimate goal in the Jesus enterprise is to share the gospel in a relevant, contemporary way. While many churches boast "contemporary" ministry, in reality, all churches are culturally relevant. Unfortunately, most churches are relevant to some other culture, some other generation, or both.[5] *Relevant* is defined by your target audience, not by yourself.

As I mentioned earlier, creating a school helped our old Anglo congregation in Detroit begin reaching our young, African American community. Not everything we tried was an instant success. After months of teaching and preaching, I was thrilled to discover our women's group also caught the vision to reach out to our community. They had decided to resurrect a program from twenty years earlier that hadn't been provided since the neighborhood had culturally changed. These wonderful and well-meaning women of German descent decided to have a neighborhood dinner and invite people to a free meal. It was outstanding! What a mission vision! Unfortunately, they decided to serve the same menu from twenty years before—knockwurst and sauerkraut! For the African American people in our community, knockwurst and sauerkraut wasn't much of a draw. It was a method that worked well fifty years earlier, when it attracted the parents and grandparents of the women in our church. But it wasn't relevant to the community we were trying to reach in *our* day.

I'll never forget visiting a missonary friend, Tony Steinbronn, in Gaborone, Botswana, Africa. We went out to the Kalahari Desert, to one of the most remote mission outreaches in the world. As we walked through the village, Tony spoke about the crucial component of relevance in religious communication. He said, "Worship is the liturgy of life. When you want to provide indigenous ministry—ministry that is in the context of the people, ministry that makes the people and you observe the liturgy of life. Then you translate that into the way you share the faith and the way you worship." That's what missionaries do. They build bridges so they can share the gospel in a *relevant* way.

Developing platforms for relevant gospel communication is crucial to your church's ability to speak in a relevant way to unchurched people. At Marble Collegiate Church in New York City, the former congregation of Dr. Norman Vincent Peale, the church has created a platform to engage those who are unlikely to ever darken the door of a church. Their ministry effort is called the New Spirit Café. It's described as a "hip kind of spiritual oasis-cum-eatery designed to feed the souls—and stomachs—of those who may be disillusioned by organized religion."[6]

Developing a platform may even signal a dress code more familiar to the unchurched. At Iron Hill Community Church in New Castle, Delaware, they developed a direct mail advertising piece that went to the community to attract young adults by promising they can wear jeans to church. Their ad says, "God doesn't require suits and ties, so why should we?"

At Hillcrest Church in Dallas, Texas, the congregation invested in a building that provides a platform for engaging the culture. Their eight thousand-square-foot performing arts center features everything from ballet to opera to gospel music. The founding pastor, Dr. Morris Sheats, calls the fine arts programs "bridge events." Their purpose is to introduce young adults to the church in a more secular context.[7] Homer McKnight, who designs and builds engaging church buildings, helped shape the Grove City Church of the Nazarene in Grove City, Ohio (www .mcknightgroup.org). The side door is large enough to drive a full-sized fire engine onto the platform for their service honoring fire-fighters. On their annual "Bikers' Sunday," thousands of motorcycle enthusiasts show up to worship, and the platform is loaded with Harleys (www.gccn.org).

Leonard Sweet reflects that the postmodern culture demands that we develop bridging ministries that engage people.

> Why was Times Square the most popular place to greet the new millennium?
> Why are coffee bars the new dating places?
> Why is the Internet becoming less a disseminator of information and more a social medium?
> Why are more and more people logging on, not to gain information but to hear, "You've got mail," and even to find love on-line?
> Why is the first thing a teen does after getting home from school is check E-mail and log on with friends?
> Relationship issues stand at the heart of postmodern culture.[8]

Yet, bridging goes beyond attracting people to a church building.

If you don't get outside the building or congregation, Christianity can remain institutional. Not everyone is going to come to the church, even to churches that create engaging ministries. As Terry Crist says,

> In recent years I have discovered that ministry happens both inside and outside the local church. For too long churches have reduced ministry down to the level of singing in the choir, teaching a Sunday school class or doing hospital visitation. As a result of this limited perspective, we have excluded many members in the Body of Christ from fulfilling ministries in the marketplace.[9]

Your church has a responsibility to train and equip you and other members to be an effective witness to your way-of-life contacts as you build relationships with friends, relatives, neighbors, and people with whom you work or go to school. Many in our world are down on institutions but high on relationships. Michael Fullan, in his book *Leading in a Culture of Change*, says,

> we have found that the single factor common to every successful change initiative is that *relationships* improve. If relationships improve, things get better.... Leaders must be consummate relationship builders with diverse people and groups—especially with people different than themselves. Effective leaders constantly foster purposeful interaction and problem solving, and are wary of easy consensus.[10]

Fullan is primarily addressing the business sector, but the same is true for you, as you reach out to non-Christians.

Communication on a relevant platform is always a challenge but indispensable for engaging ministry. Rick Warren, in his classic book *The Purpose-Driven Church*, says,

> The crowd does not determine whether or not you speak the truth: The truth is not optional. But your audience does determine *which* truths you choose to speak about. And some truths are more relevant than others to unbelievers.
>
> Can something be both true and irrelevant? Certainly! If you had been in a car accident and were bleeding to death in the emergency room, how would you feel if the doctor came in and wanted to talk about the Greek word for *hospital* or the history of the stethoscope? His information could be true, but it would be irrelevant because it doesn't stop your hurt. You would want the doctor to begin with your pain.[11]

If you or your church demonstrates irrelevance, you are doing more harm to the kingdom of God than good. Not only do people fail to hear the gospel, but they come to the conclusion (based on the irrelevant platform) that God is old, out-of-date, or on vacation in Argentina. This is a huge step back if you are trying to share the gospel with those who desperately need it. Relevance is not an option when it comes to communication of spiritual truth. Life-changing outreach will not happen without it.

Eat What Is Set Before You

When Jesus sent out his disciples for one of their first ministry training exercises, he instructed them to "eat what is set before you" (Luke 10:8). Some people may gloss over this verse thinking Jesus was just giving some dietary advice or speculate that people in that region were good cooks and the disciples should try the food. But this statement from Jesus isn't an indiscriminate suggestion. It is a basic missionary tenet about engaging the culture. It means they were not to superimpose their cultural tastes, menu, or agenda on the people they were trying to reach. They were to submit to that culture and subordinate their own comfort. Why? So the gospel would go out in a way that was incarnated (relevant) to the people they were trying to reach.

When I take people on overseas mission trips, I challenge them to apply this insight. As we visit people of various cultures, I quote Jesus and encourage them to eat what is set before them. Consequently, those of us who have been on the mission field in various cultures have eaten some strange meals—strange, that is, to our Western culture. We've eaten elephant, rhinoceros, and giraffe in South Africa and barbecued snake from the Mekong Delta for breakfast in Cambodia. My favorite challenge was for our participants to join in a meal of Mopani worms, a casserole of cooked-up grubs that are a delicacy for a people in southern Botswana. Is good mission work a challenging adventure? Whether it's different food or moving beyond the old hymnal, you bet it is!

Here's the point: Relevant gospel communication is most likely to be effective when you strip away cultural baggage and let raw Christianity take root in the other culture to find expression that is indigenous, or natural, to that culture.

Enterprise ministry gives birth to a different kind of evangelism. It is a sensitive and contextualized interaction that is more like lifestyle evangelism. Does *evangelism* scare you? Does it conjure up images of knocking on doors or shouting on street corners? Enterprise ministry goes beyond presentation-based evangelism (focused on presenting an outline supported by Bible verses). Instead, it is one-on-one witnessing through established relationships. It is sharing what God has done that makes a difference in your life.[12]

This moves evangelism in the church beyond a few people who have the gift of evangelist. All Christians, including you, can learn to share their faith one-on-one. It is powerful to relate how God has changed your life, especially when you tell your story to someone with whom you have built a relationship. Once this kind of gospel communication is shared with large numbers of people in a church, it has explosive possibilities.

When I work with people to increase their one-on-one witness potential, I ask them to develop a sociogram.

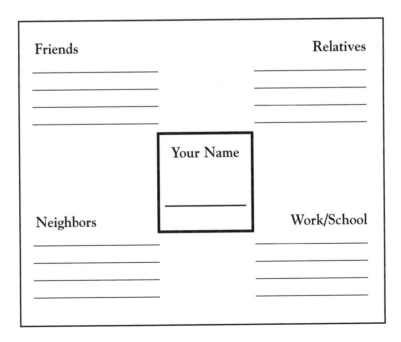

Imagine if you asked the people in your church to develop a sociogram. Their friends, relatives, neighbors, people with whom they work or go to school are people they already know. If they know them well, they are a *legitimizer* to them. Whatever they say has some credibility. Just imagine if they were to list those they know who are functionally unchurched—they don't attend a church—and you used these sociograms as a way to intentionally reach out to others? What if you regularly prayed that God would provide the opportunity to share the good news of Jesus Christ and its eternal consequences with these people? We did this when I pastored Zion Lutheran Church in Corunna, Indiana (www.kpcpages.com/?Zion_Lutheran_c). A rural church of two hundred people, we discovered we collectively knew more than three thousand people who were unchurched and lived within twenty minutes of our congregation! This could be a real harvest field for your congregation, too.

One-on-one witnessing, sharing the gospel in a relevant way through enterprise ministry, has enormous appeal in the world today. In this postmodern world, people are skeptical of religious institutions. In this information age with all its technological advances, people are networking more than ever. Consequently, relationships are more important than ever. In their book, *The One to One Future: Building Relationships One Customer at a Time*, marketing leaders Don Peppers and Martha Rogers identify for the business community what Christians should learn for outreach opportunities.[13] We live in a one-on-one world. Since technology connects people, most will receive influence from others not in mass gatherings (like inviting people to church) but, first and foremost, on a one-on-one basis. One-on-one communication, whether in the business world or sharing Christ through an enterprise ministry, happens productively in a context where the relationship is strong and felt needs are known. This is not new. In fact, the world has come full circle so that we are much more like the world Jesus encountered in his earthly ministry. Today, we can communicate as Jesus did more productively than perhaps ever before.

Relevant ministry will challenge you to connect with people at their level. Lynne and Bill Hybels reflect on Jesus' ministry in their book *Rediscovering Church*:

> Jesus was scandalously generous in distributing love. In Luke 7, when He was dining at the invitation of the Pharisees, the neighborhood prostitute barged in and fell down before Him, her tears bathing His feet. It was the social embarrassment of the month! But Jesus didn't whack her for her wicked life. He didn't throw her out to demonstrate that He hadn't had any prior acquaintance with her. He didn't sermonize on morality.
>
> Instead He looked into her eyes and discerned that her tears of repentance were genuine. Then He assured her that her moral debt had been canceled by love of another kind.
>
> Do you know the shocking message that we've got to communicate to your neighborhood and mine? *That love of another kind is still available....*
>
> We need to be reckless purveyors of saving grace. In the end, it's only this love of Christ that can change our attitudes, reshape the way we relate to others, and make us more forgiving, more generous, and more loving. Ultimately, it is this love that can turn our churches into authentic biblical communities.[14]

In Luke 15, Jesus is confronted by the religious leaders who berated him for hanging out with the "low end of society." He ate and conversed with nonreligious people, prostitutes, and tax collectors. This repulsed the religious leaders. Tim Wright comments,

> In essence, the Pharisees were saying, "This fellow is too close to culture. He welcomes sinners and hangs with them. He calls them his friends. He even acts like them. He parties too much. He drinks too much. How can he possibly call himself a religious leader when he looks, acts, and smells so much like common sinners? This man has disqualified himself from leadership."[15]

There is a risk to engaging the culture. But it is a risk worth taking. My friend Eugene Bunkowske, a brilliant missions professor, says, "It is more dangerous for the church to be cautious than for the church to be daring." What are the primary risks involved in engaging your culture and developing a platform for relevant gospel communication? I believe there are four.

1. The Risk of Temptation

When you're involved in the culture and seeing people living sinful lifestyles, there is the temptation to go beyond hating the sin and loving the sinner. Sometimes it's tempting to love the sin. There are frequent stories of pastors who were excellent counselors. However, at some point, they crossed the line in a counseling session with a person of the opposite sex who was lonely, starved for affection and in need of love. Engaging culture includes the risk of becoming a part of the culture, in the sense of falling into sin.

2. The Danger of Syncretism

Syncretism occurs when the desire to be relevant is so mixed with the culture that the truth is lost. This is the case when there is confusion between the style of the ministry and the substance of the message.[16] An example of syncretism occurred when Jesuit missionaries reached out from Europe to South America. They did a great job of sharing the Christian faith to the various tribal peoples of the continent. They were strong at packaging the message with cultural *style*. But sometimes they went too far and compromised the *content* of the faith with local customs. That is why there are pockets of Roman Catholicism in South America today where voodoo and Catholicism are intertwined. This is the result of syncretism. It is one of the risks to avoid as you engage the culture.

3. The Risk of Religious Backlash

Perhaps the greatest risk to engaging culture is religious backlash. It's what Jesus faced all the time with religious leaders. It is the criticism of fellow Christians who fail to understand your passion to engage culture. Often this backlash is directed toward pastors. When Christians engage culture, there are always those who, within the church community, lash out and criticize. They are most frequently those who themselves are ineffective at sharing the gospel with unbelievers. Often, they do not understand the primary purpose of the church, or they are more comfortable in their own ghetto of traditionalism.

Dynamic Christianity has always been risky. Thomas Aquinas claimed, "If the primary aim of a captain were to preserve his ship, he would keep it in port forever." Neil Anderson and Elmer Towns share the story of the Coast Guard captain who ordered his crew to sea during a fierce storm to rescue a sinking ship. "A frightened young seaman protested, 'We can't go out, we will never come back.' To which the old captain responded, 'We must go out, we don't have to come back.'"[17]

4. The Danger of Humanitarianism Without Gospel

A balanced enterprise ministry combines a committed focus on engaging the culture with a passion and a purpose for sharing the gospel. Such a balance can overcome the risk of humanitarianism without gospel. Remaining faithful to disciple-making as the goal results in redeeming the culture and assures that the gospel witness will not disappear in the next generation of the ministry. From the perspective of history, humanitarianism without the gospel witness has been a cancer in enterprise ministries. There is always pressure to reduce the gospel witness. In the spring of 2003, the U.S., with Great Britain, waged war on Saddam Hussein's regime in Iraq. At the close of this effort, humanitarian aid was rushed to the Iraqi people. One of the agencies providing aid was Samaritan's Purse (www.samaritanspurse.org). Samaritan's Purse food packages had a label with John 3:16 printed on them. An immediate outcry came from various groups to put pressure on Samaritan's Purse to eliminate the witness and reduce the effort to humanitarian aid alone. While the strategy (a Bible verse without relationship) can be challenged, the point is that the pressure to reduce the witness is often an issue for enterprise ministries.

Enterprise Ministries—Nothing New

The development of enterprise ministries by the Christian movement is not a new phenomenon. Throughout history, Christians have developed hospitals, schools, universities, orphanages, and many other ministries to meet the needs of people.

There are, within the development of enterprise ministries, historically verifiable risks, as mentioned above. Unless a clear focus on mission is established and continually promoted, enterprise ministries can become less directed toward eternal fruit. This is why evangelism is not enough. Discipleship is key.

While Harvard and Yale universities were primarily developed to train pastors for the mission field of a relatively young United States of America, they have developed into schools of learning that have very little connection with their original purpose. The landscape is dotted with hospitals that carry the name of various Christian organizations or denominations. They were founded with the purpose of providing medical care for people in need *and* ministering in the eternal dimension.

The YMCA, and the subsequent YWCA, were originally ministries designed to engage young people through the athletic environment. It had the purpose of witnessing the Christian faith to them and promoting an environment where the Christian faith could grow. But while today's YMCA and YWCA offer great community services, they have little resemblance to a Christian environment or witness mechanism in the context of athletics. Most are just community efforts providing a neighborhood gymnasium and other physical fitness-related programs. Somewhere in history, the movement became "messageless." If Christianity were outlawed, the YMCA and YWCA would not fear being closed. Today, enterprise ministries around athletics are being revived through the development of a sports ministry training effort embraced by over a dozen Bible colleges and a few seminaries. The movement is headed by Dr. Gregory Linville at Malone College in Canton, Ohio (www.malone.edu). Malone, a centerpiece institution in this movement, offers a four-year and a master's degree in sports ministry. The benefit of this movement is that it is training sports ministers who will be connected to churches, where discipleship can more readily occur. Parallel to this is the explosion of churches that have built family life centers. Dr. Adrian Rogers leads Bellevue Baptist Church in Cordova, Tennessee (www.bellevue.org). This church has grown significantly through the outreach provided by the family life center and numerous sports fields, which are an entry point to the church for unchurched people in the community.

Even the Salvation Army has struggled to redefine its primary mission (www.salvationarmy.org). Many homeless people find shelter, and many hungry people are fed, much to the credit of the great work of the Salvation Army. But, to quote Jesus, "Will you gain anything if you win the whole world but lose your life? Of course not! There is nothing you can give to regain your life" (Matthew 16:26).

Church-operated elementary schools in the United States, for example, were founded by many ethnic groups of Christians who came from European origins. Many of these schools were founded so that the children in a land that had a different language (English) could be educated in the ethnic heritage of their parents and grandparents from the old country. The schools were a way to continue and perpetuate the ethnicity of the group.

As the U.S. became more English-language specific, enrollment began to drop in many of these Christian schools. There was a need for revenue. Many churches opened up their schools to those who were "outsiders," allowing them to attend—if they paid tuition. Many churches called it outreach but without developing relationships "for the purpose of evangelistic efforts." They fell short of enterprise ministry potential that was available to them.

As a consultant to churches, I see many preschools and day care centers that are operated by congregations and identified as "outreach ministries." But, in truth, the workers within the average preschool or day care center do not see their efforts as outreach based. Their philosophy of ministry is to provide quality education and/or day care. Often, the mission or purpose of such an effort is to provide space that generates income for the church. It does meet a need for parents in the community. But what is the objective of the church? If the mission of the church is the rental space business, then the church is true to its purpose. But if the purpose of the church is to make disciples, then these preschools and day care centers are not consistent with the church's objective and are not mission-based Jesus enterprises. Further, they may provide a platform for relevant gospel communication, but if they don't actually communicate, the connection for eternal fruit isn't produced.

The historical trend is to get so wrapped up in meeting needs that the eternal dimensions of the ministry get lost. On the other extreme, some Christian ministries are so intent on evangelization, they fail to exercise genuine care for people *as people*. This certainly violates the strong words from James to not only talk about the faith but live it (James 1:22). The key is to have balance: Meet needs and, in that context, share the faith. That is genuine Jesus enterprise.

Enterprise ministry is *identifying and meeting felt needs in the culture, genuinely caring for others, building relationship bridges, and communicating the gospel in a relevant way*. So how are you doing at it? What changes can you make right now? What changes need to be made by the leadership at your church? In many ways, effective enterprise ministry is a reflection of its leadership. This is the subject of chapter 5.

Enterprising Thoughts

- As an enterprising Christian, you develop evangelistic opportunities by demonstrating acceptance. It's called grace.

- While the Great Commission clearly challenges you and me to "go" to people, what usually happens is that we establish a building and then focus most of our attention on inviting people to come to us.
- Sensitively identifying needs requires knowing people who are not Christians and developing genuine relationships with a listening ear and a learning attitude.
- Christianity is not so much taught or promoted as it is caught by sharing, experientially, through relationships as people are infected with the reality of your relationship with Jesus Christ.
- Enterprise ministry includes an unconditional acceptance of others.
- In reality, all churches are culturally relevant. Unfortunately, most churches are relevant to some other culture, some other generation, or both.
- If you or your church demonstrates irrelevance, people come to the conclusion that God is old, out-of-date, or on vacation in Argentina.
- Relevant gospel communication is most likely to be effective when you strip away cultural baggage and let raw Christianity take root in the other culture to find expression that is indigenous, or natural, to that culture.
- From the perspective of history, humanitarianism without the gospel witness has been a cancer in enterprise ministries.
- Enterprise ministry is *identifying and meeting felt needs in the culture, genuinely caring for others, building relationship bridges, and communicating the gospel in a relevant way.*

Next Step Questions

1. Why do churches create a subculture? How does this subculture prohibit effective outreach? What are some trappings in your church that perpetuate this?
2. What is the ultimate goal of an enterprise ministry? How does your "platform" impact your effectiveness at

communicating the gospel? What are some ways you can strengthen your platform?

3. What are some of the risks associated with enterprise ministry? Which risk(s) do you think keep people at your church from employing this kind of strategy?

CHAPTER FIVE

LEADERSHIP FOR ENTERPRISE MINISTRIES

It's not the size of the project that determines its acceptance, support, and success. It's the size of the leader.   John C. Maxwell

What's wrong with this picture: It was announcement time during the worship service and the pastor began with a plea for Sunday school teachers: "We really need volunteers to teach Sunday school. Our Sunday school is growing, and we just don't have enough teachers. So think and pray about volunteering. See Bob Johnson in the Sunday school office after church today or next Sunday. In just two weeks we'll begin a new quarter, and we'll need five more teachers to cover all the classes that we're going to provide for children."

This is a good example of leadership committed to institutional maintenance. It is the opposite of the Jesus enterprise style of ministry. How often do you hear pleas such as "We need..."?

Who is "we"? The pastor and the staff? The leadership of the church? The bureaucratic machinery? The institution? While the need certainly is valid and the challenge for volunteers is understandable, it's not the way Jesus engaged people. Even though it is the most common approach used in churches, it is not the biblical approach that characterizes the Jesus enterprise.

Jesus began with the individual, not the institution, bureaucracy, or "the need." When it came to the need for workers in the Christian movement, this was Jesus' statement: "The harvest is large, but there are few workers to gather it in. Pray to the owner of the harvest that he will send out workers to gather in his harvest" (Matthew 9:37-38). The closest Jesus got to a recruiting announcement was asking his followers to *pray* that God would send workers into his harvest—presumably, in his way. What is his way?

Jesus went up to a couple of fishermen one day. Their lives weren't about world evangelization. They weren't standing on the shore contemplating a career change from fishermen to apostles. Their lives revolved around fish. So Jesus engaged them at their level. He said, "Come with me, and I will teach you to catch people" (Matthew 4:19). He didn't recruit them on the basis of the enormous needs of the emerging Christian movement. Their first invitation to be a part of the Jesus enterprise was simply an offer to follow. And they did. They surely had no clue what they were getting into. They weren't ready! In the days and years that followed, God, in Jesus Christ, would gently engage them through interactive discussion, teaching, and demonstration of ministry. They would be discipled. There was very little emphasis on the movement, or the institution that would emerge—called the church. The focus was on individuals.

As the church did emerge, the teaching remained consistent. The leaders of the New Testament church also focused on the individual, not the institution. They engaged people in this Jesus enterprise. They discipled their followers. They helped them discover where God had called them to ministry according to their spiritual gifts.

Leadership in the Jesus enterprise is all about focusing on the individual and helping that individual find his or her destiny according to the way God provides gifts. In other words, the primary emphasis is not on filling a need in the institution but on helping a person discover their niche in the body. This is what I call *person-centered recruitment*. It is engaging people with sensitivity to their need to find their own spot on the team that God has put together, the church.[1]

Proactive Leadership

Leadership in the Jesus enterprise is predicated on a posture that engages culture. As the leadership goes, so goes the entire church. The personality of the church is greatly influenced by the personality of its leader.[2] Most unchurched people have the perception that pastors and church leaders look down on them. They feel judged. All too often, their perceptions are accurate. When you have a posture of judgment, it reflects an air of superiority.

But in the Jesus enterprise, the approach is different. Jesus was kind, gentle, meek, and full of grace, hope, and love. People were attracted to him as if he were a magnet. His posture of acceptance was something very rare in their culture. It is very rare in any culture, even today. George Grant writes, "What a terrible irony. Jesus made it plain that if the Christian community wants to have the authority to speak truth into the lives of the people around us, to give moral vision to our culture, and to ultimately shape civil justice, we must not grasp at the reins of power and prominence. Rather, we must serve. We must live lives marked by mercy."[3] Engaging leadership is strong on mercy and kindness.

Leaders *Lead*

For many congregations, the reinvention to Jesus enterprises means that some forms, styles, habits, and traditions will have to change. Whenever change is required, even in the kingdom of God, dynamic leadership is essential.

Unfortunately, many pastors believe the unbiblical myth that their role is to be an enabler. The thinking goes something like this: "You people (the masses) get together and discuss it for awhile. You decide what we should do. Then you let me know, and I will do everything in my power to make sure that it happens." This sort of democracy is not only detrimental to the church and it's mission but also has no biblical basis. It is highly influenced by democratic societies. It is not a biblical worldview. There is no evidence in scripture that this form of everybody-gets-a-vote-about-everything style of leadership is in tune with what God has in mind. If you had to label a style of government reflected in the New Testament, the church would be more like a republic. Why? Because God gifted some of his people with the spiritual gift of leadership. Further, throughout both the Old and New Testaments, it is clear that every time God had something important to accomplish, he raised up a leader. That leader led his people—without compromising by democratic voting procedures. While Jesus was meek, mild, loving, and accepting, he also was on a mission. He would not be distracted from it. Can you imagine Jesus talking to his followers, new believers, and asking them to get together and decide what he should do next?

When everyone in the congregation has the right to make a decision on where the church is going, it makes the whole congregation the leader. If that's true, who is left to do ministry? Usually the pastor, the staff, and the leaders of the church, who end up carrying out most of the ministry. This has several detrimental effects: (1) The few do the work of the many; (2) the few don't have all the gifts necessary to do all the ministry; (3) the ministry can't possibly get done because there's too much to do; (4) the few very quickly experience burnout; and, (5) the masses are robbed from the joy of being in ministry. It's a reversal of what God has in mind! God's plan is that everyone gets an opportunity to be engaged in ministry. When Jesus said, "Follow me," he was exercising his leadership. But he was also setting up an enterprise in which his followers would have the privilege and honor of being engaged in ministry.

If a church is to become a Jesus enterprise, it must have leaders who will exercise their role to guide the congregation through some challenging decisions. I consulted a Mennonite church in the conservative and somewhat rural environment of Shipshewana, Indiana. They wanted to know how they might build a campus and reach out to their community. This never would have happened if the pastor and leadership hadn't exercised their role to influence the congregation. They showed them what God was doing in the congregation and the community and shared what God was leading them to do in the future. This emphasizes a key point John Maxwell has made about facilitating change in the church. To make his point, Maxwell says, "Everything rises and falls on leadership." He claims that leaders display certain characteristics that include an entrepreneurial spirit.[4]

I worked with a church in Iowa that was growing, landlocked, and out of space. It was a no-brainer: They had to move. After some investigation, I determined there were two parcels of land that were potential relocation options for the congregation. One was smaller, hidden from the highway, and quite expensive. The other piece of land was three times larger, was on the most visible highway coming into the town, and was even more expensive than the other parcel. The purchase of the first parcel would be a stretch for the congregation, but possible. The proposed concept was that the church could build a portion of its new campus there and stay at its landlocked campus for a while. In order to get the more preferable parcel, the church would have to make a major move—selling its present property in the landlocked area of the city. The church eventually made a decision for the less preferable parcel. Why? It wasn't a money issue. It was a leadership issue. The pastor was not a strong leader. For this decision, the church needed entrepreneurial leadership.

Many pastors gravitate toward full-time ministry because they love people. That's good! But sometimes, they are focused primarily on being "people pleasers." This can become a higher priority than the purpose God has for the church. When that happens, pastors resist confrontation at all costs—a sign of ineffective or undeveloped leadership.

Without proper leadership, church people generally vote in favor of their comfort. They will lean in the direction of the status quo. There is a prevailing assumption among many Christians that God wants his people to be comfortable at all costs. Nothing could be further from biblical truth. In fact, God frequently allows discomfort so that people will grow. As Chuck Swindoll once said, "God is more interested in your character than your comfort" (www.insight.org). Jesus said very clearly, "Do not think that I have come to bring peace to the world. No, I did not come to bring peace, but a sword. I came to set sons against their fathers, daughters against their mothers. . . . Those who do not take up their cross and *follow in my steps* are not fit to be my disciples. Those who try to gain their own life will lose it; but those who lose their life for my sake will gain it" (Matthew 10:34-35, 38, emphasis mine).

Leadership has a responsibility to move beyond the status quo, to do what is right. The responsibility of Christian leadership is to influence people to move forward into unfamiliar and uncomfortable territory. Vigilant leadership is absolutely essential if a church is to become a Jesus enterprise.

John Maxwell, in his teaching on the portrait of a leader, identifies four qualities of effective leadership.[5]

1. Character

Character combines the elements of backbone and strength. Character enables the leader to rise to challenges. In every congregation that has transitioned to enterprise ministry, there were people who challenged the direction of the leadership. Virtually every church today that is reaching out and engaging its community is challenged by those who were more interested in their comfort and the status quo. Strong character allows the leadership to be more focused on what God wants rather than what some people want.

2. Perspective

The second element in the portrait of a leader is perspective. It is the leader's responsibility to cast vision and raise the level of faith for followers to make the move toward something exciting. It includes intuition and the ability to plan ahead. Years ago, there was a large parcel of land just outside of Orlando, Florida. Most of it would qualify as a swamp. Ultimately, it became Walt Disney World, one of the most amazing theme parks anywhere on the planet. On the day of dedication, someone reflected on the death of Walt Disney just a few years before. He said, "It's too bad that Walt couldn't see this." One of the Disney executives turned to the man and said, "Oh, but he did see it. That's why it's here."

One of the key elements of leadership is to help people see what does not yet exist. John Hampton, the preaching pastor of the First Christian Church of Canton, Ohio, is a man of great leadership ability and vision. John invited me to work with him and his leaders because the congregation experienced enormous growth and was running out of room on their present campus. I have watched John cast the vision to purchase a golf course and build a whole new campus, including a performing arts center. Without leadership, there is no vision. Without vision, people do not have direction (Proverbs 29:18).

3. Courage

Courage is manifested by trusting God, knowing God is present, and trusting God to bring the victory. It is perseverance with commitment. Courageous leaders are able to risk and embody a pioneering spirit.

Wayne Anderson is the pastor of First Church of God, East Central Indiana. His growing church was located on a dead-end road in a hidden portion of the small town of Eaton, Indiana. They were drawing numerous professional people from the city of Muncie, fifteen miles to the south. I recommended they relocate to the north side of Muncie. Wayne, with a strong group of leaders, made a commitment to risk and exercise a pioneering spirit to relocate the church. For several years they have used the convention center in Muncie as a temporary home while they purchased land and designed a campus that would engage their community. It would have never happened without their courage to trust God and become an enterprise ministry.

4. Favor

Favor is the combination of charisma and skills required to influence people. It is the ability that God gives those with the gift of leadership to guide and direct people with utmost sensitivity, recognizing the discomfort that comes with change. David Schieber is a senior pastor in Cordova, Tennessee (www.adventpres.com). David radiates the love of God. He is an encourager. But he is also a leader who has exercised great vision in the years of his ministry at Advent Presbyterian. He has exercised that influence in the areas of expanding worship services, building a family life center, and developing sports ministries that engage the people of the culture they are reaching. The congregation has grown dramatically. People follow David's leadership because he has strong charisma and people skills, and he influences them toward new levels of effectiveness as an enterprise ministry.

Many people have one or two of the elements in the portrait of a leader. But a catalyzing leader, according to Maxwell, has all four. Character, by itself, means you're a good citizen. Character plus perspective makes you a wise person. Character, with perspective, plus courage, is the definition of an entrepreneur. But character with perspective and courage, plus favor is an effective leader for change. This is enterprise leadership.

Leading Toward Change

Enterprise ministry requires leaders who understand the principles of change. Unfortunately, most pastors and church leaders have not been trained to be change agents. Moving a church toward enterprise ministry requires the passion and ability to be a change agent. Here are five elements of a change agent in the Jesus enterprise.

Element #1: Begin Well

Change is a process. It begins as an idea. Ideas take time to incubate, germinate, and blossom. Good enterprise change agents have sensitivity to timing. They recognize that the first stages of change are very important. It is in the beginning stages that impressions are made and attitudes are encouraged. Strategic partnerships are built between key influencers. This cultivation is very important for the change process.[6]

All too often, change is dropped on people like a bombshell. I recently worked with a Baptist church in North Carolina. Three years ago, the staff and the elders felt "led by God" to do away with the traditional service and change to two contemporary/ blended services on Sunday morning. Their motive was good. They wanted to engage a younger segment of the community. But, without cultivating the idea and processing it with the members, they simply announced their intentions and made the change. They soon faced a major rebellion in the ranks! The problem wasn't the change. The problem was that the leadership didn't honor the change principle to begin well. By the time they realized their mistake, their credibility had taken a serious hit.

Element #2: Honor Your Environment

Every church lives within an environment. Often, there is little you can do to change your environment. You have little or no control over the context in which you find your church. If you're an inner city church, you're probably always going to be an inner city church. If you're a rural church, that is the context of your ministry. There are actually two levels of your environment. (1) Contextual factors include the neighborhood or city in which you are located. There is a church in Sterling Heights, Michigan, for example, where the state condemned the property and designed a highway to go right through the sanctuary. There was little the church could do but react to that contextual factor. (2) Institutional factors, on the other hand, are factors that are tied to your own congregation. They include the tradition that you inherit and the people, with their various opinions. There is a tool, called the Church Vitality Profile, which measures contextual and institutional factors and provides a profile of the health and vitality of a church. The church is then positioned on "growth potential" and "growth probability" scales. This provides a barometer to see where a church is strong or weak in its ability to engage the culture. The Church Vitality Profile measures the circumstances within a church community that prohibit or encourage the ability to change.[7] Leaders who want to develop enterprising ministry need to understand their environment.

Element #3: Provide Good Communication

Too many leaders believe that because something appears once in the church bulletin, everyone knows about it. Good communication, particularly when it involves change, must be repeated, varied, continuous, and without assumptions. Never assume that people "get it." Use a variety of forms of communication: print, visual, formal, informal, bulletin, newsletter, Web site, verbal announcements, and so on.

The key, again, is to cast vision. Jesus knew his focus and his direction. He simply would not be deterred from it. Jesus was a man of vision. Not one day of his life did he get up, look to heaven, and say, "Well, here we go again!"

It is also important, particularly in leading toward change, to give an abundance of information. People need to have access to the details. If the communication can be put in picture form, that always helps. In his enterprise ministry, Jesus pointed to lilies in the field and told stories. To me, a graph is worth a thousand words. Too many church leaders practice mushroom management: Keep people in the dark and open up the door once in a while to throw manure on them.

It is important to correct misinformation. Remember that change is a process. People should have information in bits and pieces along the way. Don't force-feed change. Most people can't handle it. Practice processing, not event shock.

Element #4: Deal with Conflict

Within every church environment, you face conflicting situations. People will often become very emotional, sometimes even irrational, about issues surrounding the practice of their faith. That is because faith is very close to your seat of emotions. Since leadership in the Jesus enterprise requires engaging the culture, the potential for conflict rises. The environment of change and innovation is pregnant with opportunities for tension.

Mike is a leader in a United Methodist church in a suburb of Chicago. He has served on the administrative council for years and enjoys a significant amount of influence within the congregation. Marla, who is new to the church and the council, is a somewhat high-strung, opinionated young Christian. Marla is also a single parent who has struggled through an ugly divorce. Some of the tensions from that sphere of her life have spilled over into her behavior in leadership meetings at church. Even though Mike has the responsibility and influence within the council to confront Marla privately and help her with her conflictive attitude, his propensity to try to smooth out the conflict has become part of the problem instead of the solution. Allowing the situation to continue has taken much of the passion and enthusiasm from other leaders on the council. A leader in the Jesus enterprise must be willing to deal with conflict positively and immediately.

Element #5: Build a Positive Image

A few years ago, I worked with a Christian school in Lincoln, Nebraska. In the student handbook, there was a large section on rules and behavior. Students would receive points for misbehavior. If a student received a certain number of points, they were expelled from school. However, there was no reward system for doing something right. To build a positive image, which is a key ingredient to a healthy environment for a Jesus enterprise, behavior should be influenced by positive reinforcement.

People are motivated by using the gospel, not the law. Leaders who effectively lead the Jesus enterprise-style church are those who cultivate an environment where there is reward and celebration for those who display the attitudes and servanthood of an others-focused worldview.

At Community Church near Milwaukee, the context of the congregation was characterized by negativity and discouragement. While interviewing a cross section of the congregation, my analysis showed that approximately 80 percent of the comments shared by members were negative. Much of it was nit-picking, or what Jesus called, straining at gnats (Matthew 23:24 NIV). But from my objective viewpoint, the percentage of blessings within that church outweighed challenges in just about the reverse percentage balance: 80 percent of what was happening in the congregation was positive while 20 percent were challenges that required action. So why was reality so twisted? It was a leadership issue revolving around the pastoral staff and the elders. The environment was driven by the tendency to find something wrong. In the classic book *The One Minute Manager*, Kenneth Blanchard focuses on the value of positive reinforcement. He says, "Catch someone doing something right."[8] A positive image attracts people. The enterprising Jesus was committed to developing a positive image.

In churches that develop a positive image environment for enterprise ministry, some decisions are ratified by a group (board of directors, elders, congregation, staff). But in such cases, leadership should never allow any ratifying vote that provides a result of less than 85 percent "for" and 15 percent "against." If a church accepts a vote of less than 85 percent, it is a clear indication that either the timing isn't right, the leaders have not processed the decision long enough (or thoroughly enough) with the membership, the leaders have not communicated well, or, in the worst case, the leaders are outside the will of God. A vote should not be a negative action but a positive one that points toward your congregation's solidarity. A positive image is a key principle as you change toward enterprise ministry.[9]

Enterprising Thoughts

- Leadership in the Jesus enterprise is all about focusing on the individual and helping that individual find his or her destiny according to the way God provides gifts.
- Leadership in the Jesus enterprise is predicated on a posture that engages culture. As the leadership goes, so goes the entire church.
- While Jesus was meek, mild, loving, and accepting, he also was on a mission.
- "It's not the size of the project that determines its acceptance, support, and success. It's the size of the leader." (John C. Maxwell)
- Without proper leadership, church people generally vote in favor of their comfort. They will lean in the direction of the status quo.
- All too often, change is dropped on people like a bombshell.
- Good communication, particularly when it involves change, must be repeated, varied, continuous, and without assumptions.
- A positive image is a key principle as you change toward enterprise ministry.

Next Step Questions

1. How do you get people involved in ministry? Do you focus on the individual or on the institutional need? What are some ways your church could become more person-centered than need-centered?
2. What are the four qualities of effective leadership? Why are all four important? Why would an election by vote be ineffective at selecting someone with these qualities?
3. Review the five elements of being a change agent. How well do you initiate changes? Do you honor your environment? What's the level of communication? How are your conflict resolution skills? Do you have a positive image? Look at the change process and strive to sharpen the edges of your leadership.

CHAPTER SIX

LEADING THE ENTERPRISE TRANSITION THROUGH POSITIVE CHANGE

*Too often, people assume that along with the role
of leader comes the responsibility of determining
what should be done. They develop aggressive
goals. They dream grandiose dreams. They cast
grand visions. Then they pray and ask God to
join them in their agenda and to bless their
efforts. That's not what spiritual leaders do.
Spiritual leaders seek God's will, whether it is for
their church or for their corporation, and then
they marshal their people to pursue God's plan.*

Henry and Richard Blackaby

I n the last chapter, I outlined the qualities and characteristics of those God will use to engineer the Jesus enterprise in the local church. This chapter presents six keys to consider as you move your church toward positive change. Each key is challenging, but crucial for your effectiveness to engage culture, meet needs, genuinely care for others, build bridges, and communicate the gospel in a relevant way.

Key #1: Your Church Is Not Self-Sufficient

It is my perception that thousands of churches are "stuck" in mediocrity because the leadership has been unwilling to accept the value of outside help. This may be a pride issue. Leaders often feel that if they invite an "expert" to come in, it somehow diminishes their authority within the congregation. It is perceived as an admission of need for help. The truth is, bringing in outside help only enhances the authority and influence of the leader. Some churches might never use an architect if it wasn't legally required. There would be those within the congregation who would say, "We can do it ourselves," and, of course, the main motive would be to, "save money." But, of course, not using an architect would not save the congregation's resources, but waste them through a series of ill-informed decisions. The reason the law requires an architect is that the physical building of a church, if improperly built, could fall on people, and they could be injured or killed.

There is no law that requires architectural help for *ministry*. But without help, many churches (in their properly built buildings) die or are sustained at low levels of effectiveness in ministry. Pride, and the unwillingness to invest, direct leaders away from outside help.

But no church is self-sufficient. An outside consultant—an interventionist—can serve as a tremendous catalyst for change. The extra effort of an outside specialist brings momentum to the change process. This heightens the potential for success. At the same time, it minimizes the stress and tension among the congregation because it expands the awareness of ministry dynamics. The outside consultant helps the members swallow the big pills without nearly as much pain.[1]

The outside interventionist also helps the leadership see the forest *and* the trees. Sometimes you're just too close to the situation to see the obvious. Or perhaps you see the obvious but have so many choices it's difficult to prioritize. An objective outsider can help you put first things first. For example, many churches decide to change the time of worship services. In the worst case, there are those who simply make an announcement and then change the times. I tell congregations that changing the times of worship is as large a decision as relocating the congregation. It should be approached with as much seriousness, preparation, investigation, and prayer as a relocation project. Why? Because if you change the time of worship, you're interfering with everyone's bladder (and when they eat, read the newspaper, and meet for lunch at grandma's house)!

But even in churches where the leaders study the issue of changing worship services more carefully, they still miss the big picture. They may commit it to prayer. They may interview the members to see how a change in worship time would affect their lives. But while this approach is heading in the right direction, I have yet to see a congregation that takes the next step: asking for the opinions of unchurched people in the community. If your goal is to reach them, wouldn't it be important to know when they would most likely attend worship?

Another dynamic that supports the use of an outside expert is access to the experience of that consultant. When you engage this kind of help, you tap the cumulative knowledge from many different churches. Who has the opportunity to visit hundreds of churches every year? The consultant not only visits different congregations every week for purposes of intervention but also receives ideas and identifies new and innovative ways they are reaching their communities. The truth is that most people can't gain that cumulative knowledge because they don't have the opportunity to visit so many different churches. But an outside expert brings that wealth of information to the table. You must first recognize that your church is not self-sufficient.

One of the greatest dynamics of using an interventionist is that it insulates you as a leader from negative reaction. For example, a few years ago I worked with an ELCA (Evangelical Lutheran Church in America) church in Elkhorn, Nebraska. They were growing rapidly and had maximized their facilities. The church was landlocked on a very small, fully occupied block. In order to expand with a contiguous campus, they would have to obtain a city ordinance to close a road and then purchase a number of homes, which weren't for sale. The leadership suspected I would recommend they relocate—and I did. I remember when I shared this with the membership during the report. There was a small group of people who couldn't believe that the congregation would possibly abandon its "wonderful" building. In reality, the facilities were no longer an asset to the church. This group also objected that there would be no one to buy their building, and besides, it would be difficult to find an ideal location. But I had found a location that was highly visible and accessible that would be, in my perception, nearly perfect. The following year, it turned out the city was interested in buying their property, and the location I suggested was purchased. They built and exploded with growth. As often happens, their growth presented a whole new set of challenges, and they requested another consultation. But some of the people were still bitter because I was the one who suggested they leave their "wonderful" building. So when the leadership asked for outside help, we sent one of my associates. The point is, some of the people were still bitter *at me*, not at the staff or the leadership. In that way, I was able to insulate the leadership from the negative reaction of the few disgruntled people. The proverb says, "Plans fail for lack of counsel, / but with many advisers they succeed" (Proverbs 15:22 NIV). It's true; realize you're not self-sufficient.

Key #2: Change Is Threatening!

Change of any kind is a threatening experience. It is a natural reaction to be comfortable with "the way we've always done it."

That's why one of the most common phrases in many churches is, "But we've always done it that way."

There are two aspects of change that, if understood, can make transitioning to enterprise ministry a lot easier in your church. The first is from the receiver's side. For those who are faced with change, the resistance is often connected with a failure to con-sider what God wants. Our research shows that large percentages of active Christians are more focused on what *they* want than on what *God* wants.[2] Even though Christians regularly pray the Lord's Prayer, which includes the request, "your will be done on earth as it is in heaven," when it comes to making decisions, many Christians tend to focus on what *they* want (Matthew 6:10b). Often, the question of whether the change is God's will isn't even raised or considered!

The second aspect that contributes to this challenge comes from the leader's side. Many leaders in churches tend to make changes by subtraction, which is a major mistake. Change is a lot less threatening if you follow this very simple principle: Always change by addition, never by subtraction. Here is an example: An RCA (Reformed Church in America) congregation in southeast Florida had been declining for some time, and the mood within the congregation was not good. It became obvious to me that many of the people were threatened by the suggestion of any change. Why? Because, from past experience, change was extremely painful. As I began to inquire, I discovered several instances where major changes were made to the worship service. On one occasion, the pastor had gone to a conference and learned something about contemporary worship styles. For years, his church had followed a fairly liturgical and formal style of worship. Upon his return, the pastor and the leadership decided to be bold (and somewhat foolish) by announcing "the end of the worship service as you know it," and the beginning of a new worship ser-vice starting the next week. I wasn't surprised to hear that worship attendance fell by 40 percent over the next few months, in spite of the fact that the contemporary service did attract new families in the community and reactivate some inactive members.

The pastor's and leaders' mistake was not the insertion of a contemporary worship service. It was the failure to add that service as an option while leaving the present service intact. They followed the principle of subtraction rather than addition. Here's the point: Don't ever shoot an old program. Even if it's dwindling, let it die a natural death. It's a simple, but profound, way of softening the pain of change, which is always a threatening experience.

Key #3: Change May Require Some Blood Transfusions in Leadership Positions

Sometimes the leadership has to change in order for a congregation to move into enterprise ministry. During an interview with the senior minister of a charismatic church in San Diego, he indicated that he wanted me to tell him if he was part of the problem. He said, "Maybe I've taken this congregation as far as I can with my leadership skills and gifts. Maybe it's time for new leadership. I don't want to do anything to hold the congregation back." I assured that pastor that I would do that, if necessary. The pastor can be a leadership blockage. Sometimes it's members who become negative roadblocks, who need to move on or change. Occasionally, the leadership needs to hear an admonishing word from an objective outsider. They need to change or move elsewhere. The saying may sound harsh, but it's true: "Some churches are just one transfer away from spectacular growth!"

For St. Paul Episcopal Church, located in rural east Texas, the roadblock was a man named John. John had been an active member of St. Paul his entire life. He had never married and had few hobbies. Outside of his work as a teacher, he spent most of his energy serving the church. And he was great, for many years. But he grew older, and as the church needed new, fresh strategies, John became resistant. He wasn't belligerent or evil in his resistance. He simply expressed his opinion as he always had. However, because he was practically an institution at St. Paul, no one dared oppose him. Without realizing it, John was a deterrent to the future growth of the church he loved and had faithfully served. The church was stalled. Two or three parish priests came and went. And then, in the second year of a new priest's ministry, John died. *And it literally marked a turnaround era for the church.* Isn't that a sad legacy for John, who had served his church faithfully for years but became resistant late in life?

As you seek to engage culture in an enterprise ministry, you must face this fact: Sometimes it requires a blood transfusion in leadership positions for change to occur.

Key #4: It Requires Persistence to Establish Innovation

If your church is self-centered and not engaging the culture, turning it into a Jesus enterprise will take significant effort and persistence. It is perhaps this persistence that is one of the greatest prices to pay in leadership.

The New Testament idea of leadership carries the concept of perseverance (Hebrews 13:7). God understands: If you're going to lead in the Jesus enterprise, it's going to take perseverance. Winston Churchill once spoke about persistence in a commencement address he was asked to give at Harrow School, from which he graduated as a youth. His address included one profound statement: "Never give in, *never, never, never, never.*" One of the keys to leadership in the Jesus enterprise is to have persistence and commitment that rise above seasons of adversity.

Key #5: Avoid Being Manipulated

As I visit churches, I see many leaders who are trapped by the intimidation, influence, or even positive relationships within the church. In ministry work, relationships are obviously important. It is easy for pastors to become friends with people in the congregation. But it's also common to see the entanglement of relationships, and even family blood ties within congregations, making differing opinions more challenging in the face of important change.

As a leader, you cannot allow yourself to be ruled by strong-willed people. You cannot be intimidated by people who are financially powerful. You cannot be persuaded away from God's direction by people who are longtime friends. That doesn't mean you want to remain aloof, but you must uphold God's purposes, even if it means suffering discomfort in your personal relationships.

A church in Lexington, Kentucky, had a very powerful woman in the congregation. Her heart, in many ways, was in the right place. She loved the Lord and was a faithful and loyal servant in her church. She was also very wealthy. When her husband died, she gained control of the financial empire he had built. At one point in the congregation's history, the church was running out of space in their rented facilities and began looking for a location so they could build. This woman wanted to be part of the solution but knew very little about the proper location of the church for future growth. She donated some property to the church, but the location was absolutely terrible! She meant well when she gave the gift, but because of her wealth and influence on the congregation, no one had the leadership strength to point out the inadequacy of the location.

So who was the problem? Not the woman. She meant well. The problem was the leadership at the time. They allowed themselves to be dependent and intimidated by this woman's power. They lacked the courage to ask her to sell the property and donate the proceeds toward the purchase of a better site. The church was in a dead-end situation for the following three generations. It never would have happened if the leadership had been more responsive to God's approval than to the wealthy woman's influence. Incidentally, today, as you turn off the main road to go to that church, the road sign, right next to the sign pointing the way to the church, says, "Dead End." How appropriate!

Key #6: Change Is Costly

Jesus told the parable of the man who started building without first counting the cost. The Lord indicated it was a big mistake (Luke 14:28-30). Before you start the process of becoming an enterprise ministry, make sure you are confident about the direction in which God is calling you. *Confidence* literally means, "with faith." Make sure you have faith in God to complete the calling he has given to you.

Sooner or later, your leadership toward the Jesus enterprise will cost you.[3] Michael Slaughter is senior pastor of Ginghamsburg United Methodist Church in Tipp City, Ohio, a congregation that has grown dramatically over the last several years. In his book *Spiritual Entrepreneurs*, Slaughter talks about the price of leadership.

> There is a price that goes with leadership. The leader will not be on everyone's most-liked list. Leadership means risk and change, and many people resist change. It is easier to maintain the status quo. The leader who comes to a church and begins talking about moving forward and using new wineskins will be perceived by many as a boat rocker.... The leader moves through life demonstrating the passion for which it is worth dying. Leaders are willing to pay the price. They are fully invested. They have committed their resources and energy to the purpose for which God has called them.[4]

Make sure you define your self-esteem in Christ. Many church leaders put way too much of their self-esteem in what people think or say about them. You must be clear that what God has called you to do is more important than what others think of you. The apostle Paul described the Jesus enterprise as a contest. It requires the discipline of an athlete. There is a price to pay for victory. The apostle Paul encourages you to run the race with determination—because it's worth it (1 Corinthians 9:24).

Continue to build a sense of community. Building relationships is the foundation for processing change. When people know you, they will know they can trust you. When they know they can trust you, they are much more willing to follow you.

Finally, allow God to give you strength and power to do whatever it takes. The church today is in desperate need of leadership. God needs people like you to have a passion for those in the world who do not yet know God. God needs people like you to challenge and lead others to move from maintenance ministry to an enterprise ministry that will engage the culture and change the world. God needs people like you who are motivated to accomplish the mission God has given to the church. Remember, motivated people motivate people.

Enterprising Thoughts

- An outside consultant—an interventionist—can serve as a tremendous catalyst for change.
- Change of any kind is a threatening experience.
- Even though Christians regularly pray the Lord's Prayer, which includes the request, "your will be done on earth as it is in heaven," when it comes to making decisions, many Christians tend to focus on what *they* want.
- Always change by addition, never by subtraction.
- Never shoot an old program. Let it die a natural death.
- If your church is self-centered and not engaging the culture, turning it into a Jesus enterprise will take significant effort and persistence.
- Sooner or later, your leadership toward the Jesus enterprise will cost you.
- Motivated people motivate people.

Next Step Questions

1. Review the six keys for positive change. Which areas tend to be overlooked? Why is communication one of the most important aspects in the change process?
2. How can a blood transfusion in the leadership lead to lasting change in your church? Why do you think some leaders—who may be wonderful people—can become roadblocks to their church's growth?
3. Why is change so important? What are some of the costs of change? What are the payoffs? Which are more important?

CHAPTER SEVEN

SELLING OUT? MONEYCHANGERS IN THE TEMPLE

There is too much of a tendency to have a poverty mentality in today's Church. Our outlook is too small, but the smallness can be shaken off in answer to our Lord Jesus, who has called us to be big people. Big in our worldview. Big in our love for the lost. Big in our giving. Jack Hayford

For many pastors and church leaders, money is a nasty five-letter word. I've heard pastors brag, "I never preach about money." That's a bogus boast! That's not preaching the whole counsel of God. Money was one of Jesus' most frequent topics of instruction. Money is your crystallized sweat. Much of what you do and who you are revolves around your work, which usually yields money, which translates into acquired goods and services that reflect your lifestyle. Activities, plans, aspirations—most aspects of your world—pertain to money. It can also be a huge stumbling block that keeps Christians from engaging their culture.

Christianity is catching. It is a "holy infection." But sometimes the way we do church has a way of insulating that holy infection. That removes God's people from the culture and quarantines them in a Christian subculture—an antiseptic world. And, there is perhaps no greater separation from culture than in the area of finances. Jesus enterprises meet needs in the community. Yet some are not strategically connected to local churches.

Two great examples of popular ministries meeting felt needs are Christian radio stations and Christian bookstores. Most of these ministries are not connected to a local church. While managers of Christian radio stations and owners of Christian bookstores might agree that God's mechanism for reaching the world is the local church, most of these enterprises (whether commercial or nonprofit) are physically located away from a local church. Opportunities for developing relationships, transitioning people into a community of believers, discipling them for Kingdom impact, and connecting them with other Christians are lost by the millions every day.

My foray into the world of Christian radio, through the radio program *The Church Doctor*, has been both challenging and enlightening. It quickly became apparent to me that most Christian radio stations are far from being partners in ministry with the local church. And most local churches are just as significantly uninvolved in pursuing partnerships with local Christian radio stations. My involvement with National Religious Broadcasters has helped me understand that while there is a strong degree of emphasis on influencing the political power brokers of the nation, there is very little emphasis on partnering with the local church. In fact, this topic has been one of the points of tension concerning the philosophy and direction of the National Religious Broadcasters.[1]

Christian radio is a natural extension of the church and should be closely connected to it. That connection includes where the station is located as well as how it is financed. Christian radio should receive financial support from the church as a mission expense. Peggy and Jon Campbell of Ambassador Advertising

Agency in Fullerton, California, which syndicates many top Christian radio programs, agree. The church should see Christian radio as a twenty-four-hour supplement to the preaching and teaching of the congregation. The radio station carries out the work of the church by providing spiritual support, encouragement, and outreach beyond the congregation's property lines. The same could be said of Christian television, newspapers, and magazines.

Likewise, Christian bookstores are an extension of the Christian community's resources, especially since the terrorist attacks of September 11. Since then, the hunger and search for spiritual truth, meaning to life, security, hope, and other spiritually related issues have driven many people to seek spiritual literature. These resources are an extension of the church's mission. But few Christian bookstores, whether located in a shopping mall (which is an excellent place to engage the community) or on the church campus, are an intentional Jesus enterprise of any church (or group of churches). In most Christian bookstores, there is little or no communication about any local church! Regardless of the geographic proximity of the bookstore to the church, the philosophy of ministry and training of those who operate the store has the greatest impact on how they capitalize on the engagement process for the sake of the church's mission.

That is not to say that many owners of Christian radio stations and Christian bookstores are not mission-minded. Many are. But if they are 95 percent effective at engaging the culture, yet still have a 5 percent gap because there is no intentional connection with the local church, the effectiveness is crippled for the bookstores, the radio stations, and the local church. If you believe the Jesus enterprise leads to discipleship in the community of the church, the 5 percent gap equals 95 percent ineffectiveness for the Great Commission! The few exceptions who do have close ties to a local church are pioneers and models for the rest. They can direct the people they're engaging toward the community of believers where they can be nurtured and discipled.

Why does a church often resist a connection with an enterprise ministry like a Christian radio station or bookstore? All too often, the reason is money. On one hand, the entrepreneurial nature of these efforts makes church leaders uncomfortable because they see any potential profitability as somehow diametrically opposed to the "spirituality" of the mission. On the other hand, many church leaders see these enterprise ministries as siphoning finances from the local church. Rather than challenging the members of their church to invest discretionary dollars for resources or a share-a-thon at a radio station, they would rather see it given "to the church." Ironically, this kind of thinking limits some of the dynamic ministry potential of the church.

Enterprise ministries like Christian radio and bookstores give *back* to churches through their influence in the lives of growing Christians. Melissa Montana is General Manager at STAR 88.3 in Fort Wayne, Indiana (www.star883.org). She points out: "As members are challenged, educated, and moved by these resources, they become stronger Christians." *Stronger Christians support their churches with greater generosity.*

Value

When talking about enterprise ministries, it is essential to discuss the idea of value. When a Christian church meets a felt need, especially in a culture with available resources, people will be willing to pay for that felt need to be met. Christian schools, hospitals, preschools, and day care centers have been examples of enterprise ministries that meet a felt need. *In fact, when people are willing to pay for a ministry, it is an indicator that the church is, indeed, meeting a felt need!* People pay for what they value. Unfortunately, this raises a heavy indictment against the church: Much of what the church does is perceived by people outside the church as having relatively little value.

Why doesn't the church recognize this? If you asked the typical theologian if non-Christians place a high value on what the church is doing, his or her response would be, "Of course not. They don't know the value of the gospel because they are nonbelievers." That's bad in itself. But then the theologian teaches the pastor, who leads the church, who directs the people—in a ministry that is irrelevant to unbelievers. This puts the responsibility of recognizing the value of the gospel squarely on the unbeliever. That isn't biblical! Is this what Jesus would have done?

The whole concept of mission begins with the fact that Jesus was sent into a world of people who couldn't care less. The Bible says sin clouds us from the answer to our deepest need (Romans 1:18). But Jesus bridges the gap by going *to* people—where they are—meeting their needs, developing a platform, and establishing relationships to share the gospel in a meaningful way. If that mission genuinely meets a felt need, people *will* pay for it, whether they have come to the place in their spiritual journey where they understand the gospel or not. Their payment (in dollars, time, or energy investment) is confirmation that the church has provided an enterprise ministry relevant to the culture.

Think for a moment about the Christian elementary school, an enterprise ministry mentioned earlier. The fact that the school collects tuition from parents (and should provide scholarships for those who cannot afford it) isn't a roadblock for the gospel to penetrate their lives and the lives of their children. In fact, it creates an outreach to the community that the church otherwise might not be able to afford. It is a "break-even" enterprise that engages people. Parents and students meet not only the teachers and assistants but also the pastors and, when it's truly effective, Jesus Christ.

Is this involvement in financial enterprise evil? Is this something Jesus would rebel against, like the moneychangers in the Temple? Or, does this fall under the parable Jesus told about the shrewd manager in Luke 16? Jesus concluded: "As a result the master of this dishonest manager praised him for doing such a shrewd thing; because the people of this world are much more shrewd in handling their affairs than the people who belong to the light" (Luke 16:8).

Ministry Boundaries

Are there dangers? Can pure ministry motives wind down the slippery slope toward greed? Can the mission get lost in the busyness of the effort? Absolutely! All of these dangers are very real. I consulted a church near Houston, Texas that supported a preschool directed by Betty Register. Betty had an incredible passion for reaching the lost for Jesus Christ. Unfortunately, she had trouble staffing the preschool with people who shared her passion for the mission to reach not only children but also their parents. While there was interaction on a superficial level, there was little or no relationship-building, faith-sharing, or disciple-making. Betty said, "We have such a hard time finding properly trained Christian workers who have a commitment to the mission of our church. Therefore, we have to go outside the church and employ college students. But they, too, know little of the mission to reach these children and their families for Jesus Christ and bring them into the church." One of Betty's greatest challenges for years was the lack of support from the pastors. In spite of this, the preschool was very successful.

Betty's preschool and day care program is similar to many in churches that are 95 percent outstanding enterprise ministry, yet fall the crucial 5 percent short. If Betty could multiply her worldview in every classroom, her ministry would be a much stronger Jesus enterprise. If she had more support from her pastor and her church, she could do it. How unfortunate!

Religious Commercialism

As mentioned earlier, enterprise ministries—if they are in a culture where people have resources and if they are truly centered on a felt need—can operate in a dollars-for-services trade. They can attract an income stream that pays for the ministry. This is nothing new to Christian churches; school tuition, day care fees, even paying musicians at a wedding are common. What about commercialism in the church?

Mark 11:15-18 records an event in Jesus' life that, at first glance, may seem a contradiction to enterprise ministry. During the final week of his life, he went into the Temple and began driving out all those who were buying and selling merchandise for Temple sacrifices. This event did not have the characteristics of peaceful religiosity. Jesus was angry! He overturned the tables operated by the moneychangers and went after those who sold pigeons. He said, "It is written in the Scriptures that God said, 'My Temple will be called a house of prayer for the people of all nations.' But you have turned it into a hideout for thieves!" (Mark 11:17). Jim Cymbala, pastor of the Brooklyn Tabernacle, reflects on this story, "Jesus is not terribly impressed with religious commercialism. He is concerned not only *whether* we're doing God's work, but also *how and why* we're doing it."[2]

It is my perception that Jesus would approach, with anger (righteous indignation), many preschools, elementary schools, and day care ministries that are accepted by virtually everyone. Why? Because while they provide a service, they monumentally fail to connect people with Jesus through evangelistic efforts. They have the platform to share the gospel but are not cultivating or using it for the purposes of mission. They are focusing on making money, not making disciples. Without evangelistic activity, they violate the Christian mission and commit the moneychanger "infraction." As Cymbala points out, Jesus is not just concerned about whether we are doing some type of God's work, but *how* and *why*.

Unless relationships are cultivated, the gospel is shared, and disciples are made, these seemingly good efforts only masquerade as Jesus enterprises. They are similar to the parable of the talents where each servant was given an asset to grow for the master. While the servants that were rewarded were the ones who multiplied the investment, the most despicable servant hid the asset in the ground. This servant would be the church that sits on an endowment when people all around are going to hell without Jesus. When I consulted Immanuel United Church of Christ in West Bend, Wisconsin, I met Pastor James Eckblad. He is a courageous leader trying to get his congregation to move from maintenance to mission. In the process, he had to confront a small group in the church who held on to an endowment fund so tightly when the church so desperately needed funds for Jesus enterprise ministries. As an outside interventionist, I had the opportunity to come alongside James and his leaders and remind this small group that the church is not a bank.

Those who operate preschools, day cares, elementary schools, endowments, and similar ministries without incorporating an evangelistic strategy are like the servant who did something for the master but did not clarify the *how* and *why*. While these ministries are accepted as the status quo, they fall short of enterprise ministry.

A Matter of Motive

In mission enterprises, the primary issue is *not* how much money you bring into the church (although those finances are helpful) but how well you engage the culture, build bridges, genuinely care for people, cultivate relationships, and share the gospel. If your motivation is to compensate for poor giving habits, the enterprise ministry will become a crutch and contribute to the demise of the church. A church I consulted in southern Illinois has an endowment of more than one million dollars but very poor giving by the relatively wealthy members. Those poor giving habits, coupled with little outreach, is resulting in a dying congregation. In the same way, an enterprise ministry can be dangerous unless it is paralleled with sound biblical stewardship on the part of the congregation.

On the subject of motive, there is another danger to consider. One of the top complaints of unchurched people is, "All the church wants is my money." Where does this accusation come from? Is it fair? Is it accurate? Most *Christians* would say people outside the church think the church only wants their money because they've heard too many televangelists begging for financial resources on TV. But that isn't the right answer. For one thing, unchurched people don't watch televangelists. They're not interested in any of the content, and the atmosphere of distrust keeps them from spending any serious time watching televangelism programming. Unchurched people dismiss most media evangelists as hawkers, weirdos, and fanatics. So where do people outside the church get this concept that all the church wants is their money?

After years of studying the church and unchurched people, it is my perception that the greatest "moneychanger infractions" of the local church are actually historically accepted, time-honored, "sacred" traditions. They reflect bad habits that stem from improper motives. See if you can identify the problem in the scenario below.

Rick and Julie are a young couple who have lived near Trinity Church for years. They do not attend church and have never received an invitation from Trinity to worship with them. But some of their friends attend Trinity, including Dave and Holly, who live next door. During barbecues and get-togethers they've occasionally talked about church. But Dave and Holly have never engaged Rick and Julie at the point of their felt needs.

Ironically, the church has ministry activities that would meet some of their felt needs. For instance, Rick and Julie struggle with raising their three rambunctious sons. The church offers parenting classes for people with young children. Rick and Julie are deep in credit card debt. Trinity offers a class called "Developing a Budget that Works for You," a course based on biblical wisdom. But as great as those programs are, Rick and Julie have never been invited by Dave and Holly, even though they live next door.

Now it's time for the annual spaghetti dinner at Trinity, sponsored by the youth group to gather funds so they can go on their annual ski trip to northern Michigan. Dave and Holly have a teenage girl, Wendy, who is in the youth group. Of course, they want the spaghetti dinner to be a raving success. So, with great enthusiasm and energy, they walk over to Rick and Julie's and invite them to the spaghetti dinner. To Rick and Julie, the invitation was expected (Dave and Holly had invited them last year). It's a nice thing to do, so they go. However, subconsciously, it becomes clear: In the context of church, Dave and Holly aren't really interested in Rick and Julie spiritually. Subconsciously, to Rick and Julie, it appears—in the absence of any other approaches from the church—the congregation is only interested in their contribution. It's not surprising that many unchurched people think the church is more interested in their finances than in their faith.

While enterprise ministries *can* generate income, their motive should be guided by the desire to meet genuine felt needs (of others, not the institutional needs). Then they don't run as much risk of committing the "moneychanger infraction." It all goes back to motive and mission. It is not just *whether* you do God's work, but *how* and *why*.

Can your church sponsor an annual bazaar and operate it as an enterprise ministry? Perhaps. Can the youth spaghetti dinner become a genuine enterprise ministry? Maybe. But only if they begin with a motive that has a concern for others. That motivational framework will totally reshape the purpose for the event. That, in turn, will reengineer the methodology, fulfillment of outreach opportunities, sensitivity to strategic relationship-building, sharing of the gospel, and invitations into the Christian community toward the end of making disciples. The way the event is packaged and communicated will be totally different. The driving force will be to meet the needs of people like Rick and Julie, not fill the coffers of the local church.[3]

Here's an example. Our Saviour Church sponsored a car wash by the youth. How was it a unique enterprise? It was free for anyone who did *not* belong to the church. As cars waited in line, the pastor and some church members chatted with people in their cars and offered them literature about Jesus and an engraved invitation to worship. What about members of Our Saviour Church who wanted a car wash? They paid double what it would have cost at a professional car wash. The purpose for the proceeds was well communicated to the members. The money would go to purchasing the literature handed out to non-Christians that day.

How do you keep your enterprise ministry from becoming a profit-centered business? How do you keep it from influencing the church in a way that undermines its commitment to the Great Commission? One of the congregations that has harnessed the power of enterprise ministries is Community Church of Joy (CCOJ) in Glendale, Arizona, a suburb of Phoenix. They have diagrammed their structure, not as a hierarchical traditional model, but as a flat organization that distinguishes enterprise ministries as separate but connected.

At CCOJ, the traditional church activities are identified as Services, Education, and Congregational Life. Even in these three areas, CCOJ has introduced a few enterprise ministries, although they are more traditional in nature. An example of this is that while the K-12 school and early childhood education department are traditional ministries, they also fall under our definition of enterprise endeavors.

To clearly define and organize more of its self-sustaining enterprises, CCOJ has developed the Enterprise category. They have also incorporated the Joy Company, which has several nonprofit subministries. There is also a close connection with the executive center. This is something I don't often see in churches. When that connection is missing, churches end up with an enterprise ministry with no leadership support or involvement. There is also close interaction between the other ministries and the Enterprise Circle. This is what Walt Kallestad, senior pastor at Community Church of Joy, calls "creating a profit center." He explains,

> The idea of profit centers to support the mission of nonprofit organizations is not a new idea in nonreligious circles, but it has yet to catch on in a big way with churches. Developing profit centers that are compatible and consistent with your mission is essential for building dynamic, growing centers for mission in the twenty-first century. There is simply too much to do. Congregations who are dramatically expanding their reach into the world [engaging the culture] in ways that are effective and meaningful [meeting felt needs] will demand more resources than they will get in the Sunday offering plate.[4]

Architect David Price and I have worked with Bethel Lutheran Church in Hudson, Wisconsin (www.bethelhudson.org). Under the visionary leadership of senior pastor Dennis Nelson, the church purchased a large parcel of land for a second campus. This will eventually relieve the pressure from their landlocked site in town and will also provide a highly visible and extremely accessible location to become a regional church. The church is financially challenged because even though they received the land at a significant discount, the debt load is still heavy. Because of the excitement and potential, Bethel wanted to start their campus at the new site sooner rather than later. Based on our research of the area, we identified two enterprise ministries that won't cost them at all. First, they will contract with a cell tower company, which will provide monthly income for years. Of course, this begs the question: Who would want an ugly cell tower on their church campus? Bethel will be using a tower that will be disguised as a bell tower with a computerized sign, establishing their presence at the new site. Thousands of motorists will see it every day. Second, our research identified a severe need for preschool and day care. This second, self-sufficient enterprise ministry will be part of the immediate first phase of the campus. Isn't this part of the shrewd approach that Jesus had in mind?

Another structural way that Christian ministries are insulating themselves from financial entanglements is through the use of firms that intervene in the financial process. My friend Tim Tewes is executive vice-president of FACTS Management Company in Lincoln, Nebraska (www.factsmgt.com). This is a tuition collection firm that works for nonprofits. For a small fee, they serve as the go-between for church schools (including Christian universities) and tuition-paying parents and students. This is an excellent idea, and the cost of administration is passed on to the user. The collection of user fees by a distant firm insulates the ministry from difficult situations (like collecting late fees) that might interfere with ministry opportunities. Tim and his company support Jesus enterprises.

Insulating money from the risk of misunderstood ministries is important. For example, counseling a troubled marriage between unchurched people who send their children to a Christian school may be the platform for church staff to engage a couple and share the gospel. But the platform wouldn't exist if they didn't have a relationship with the church through the school. The school provides a bridge into their family and the troubled marriage triggers the felt need that provides the platform for sharing the gospel. The insulating "safety mechanism" in the financial area is provided by the distant company, FACTS Management, that collects the tuition.

Enterprise ministries are not moneychangers in the Temple. The merchants selling the doves and coins for the Temple tax didn't care about the people purchasing their wares. The motive of enterprise ministry is to engage people by meeting their needs and offering them something of value: first meeting their temporal need and, ultimately, offering them the incomparable value of the gospel of Jesus Christ.

Enterprising Thoughts

- Christian radio, television, and bookstores are a natural extension of the church and should be closely connected to it.
- Stronger Christians support their churches with greater generosity.
- When people are willing to pay for a ministry, it is an indicator that the church is, indeed, meeting a felt need. People pay for what they value!
- "Jesus is not terribly impressed with religious commercialism. He is concerned not only *whether* we're doing God's work, but also *how and why* we're doing it." (Jim Cymbala)
- The greatest "moneychanger infractions" of the local church are actually historically accepted, time-honored, "sacred" traditions.

Next Step Questions

1. Do you see finances as a catalyst for mission or a roadblock to it? How can a Christian worldview of good stewardship influence the effectiveness of mission?
2. What are some of the dangers that can occur when a ministry loses its focus? How is it possible for pure motives to become tarnished by greed?
3. Do you agree that traditional fundraisers can communicate the wrong message to unchurched people? What are some creative ways to raise funds that also meet needs of non-Christians and engage them for Jesus Christ?

CHAPTER EIGHT

SHOW ME THE MONEY!

There is no shortage of money in the church.
There is a shortage of good stewardship.
Waldo Werning

Financial Challenges

Finances are an ongoing challenge for any church that is committed to outreach. The start-up cost of an enterprise ministry endeavor usually isn't recuperated for years— sometimes never. Likewise, the more effective a ministry becomes, the more funding is required to sustain it. But I've found that giving increases when you are involved in dynamic outreach ministry. You get excited about mission, not maintenance. As a result, your church's health and vitality increases as it focuses on others.

One of the most amazing principles to remember regarding stewardship is this: You give as you know and believe, not as you are able.[1]

Giving is always a faith issue. It's solely dependent on your world view about money. There are six stewardship principles that, if followed, would make an enormous impact on the financial situation of churches. These six principles are important for biblical stewardship and will also prevent successful enterprise efforts from becoming a crutch and undermining the vitality of the church.

1. Proportionate Giving

Our research shows that in most congregations, only 35 percent of Christians give proportionately.[2] Proportionate giving is based on a percentage not a dollar amount. But most Christians see their giving as tossing twenty dollars into the collection, which may be what they've *been* giving for years! If proportionate giving were understood and practiced, it would have a greater influence on the income of a church than the median income of its members. In other words, a lower income congregation in which large numbers of people give proportionately is more likely to be financially viable than an upper class congregation where few members think or give proportionately. The overall wealth of the members is not as strong of an economic indicator as proportionate giving.

Furthermore, the biblical teaching of proportionate giving has an exponential impact over time. As people succeed in their careers, they tend to achieve more earning power. Those who think of giving in dollar amounts tend to give proportionately less as their income rises. Those who understand proportionate giving donate more as they advance in their careers. Why? As they make more money, they are giving the same percentage of a larger income. The margin of difference between the first scenario and the second, over a period of twenty years and multiplied by two hundred church members, is phenomenal! Translated into dollars, it would astound most pastors and church leaders. The power of this principle should be no surprise; it's God's directive. This is the financial side of the Jesus enterprise. If congregations would invest in ongoing training in proportionate giving as a lifestyle, the impact on their financial welfare would amaze them. What does your church do?

2. Firstfruits Giving

In several instances, the Scriptures talk about giving to God first. First Corinthians 16:2 says, "Every Sunday each of you must put aside some money, in proportion to what you have earned." In some translations, "Sunday" means "on the first day of the week." This is another way of teaching firstfruits giving. When firstfruits giving is adopted as a general stewardship principle and financial lifestyle, it has significant impact on the financial giving in a church. God honors faith, and firstfruits giving is an act of faith. Giving off the top is your testimony of trust that God will supply all your needs. To hold back and "see how the bills end up," shows no demonstration of faith. Firstfruits giving powerfully reflects Jesus' words, "Be concerned above everything else with the Kingdom of God and with what he requires of you, and he will provide you with all these other things" (Matthew 6:33).

Giving off the top, as an act of worship, reflects a relationship of trust with Jesus, who says, "It is God who clothes the wild grass—grass that is here today and gone tomorrow, burned up in the oven. Won't he be all the more sure to clothe you?" (Matthew 6:30). Again, if this essential biblical principle isn't clear among the members of a church, an enterprise ministry, which has the potential to bring income into the congregation, could "soften" the stewardship integrity of the members. Think of the healthy scenario in your church, however, with sound biblical and financial principles *and* enterprise ministries. The result is a healthy balance, a good supply of resources from offerings, enterprise income streams, and an impact in your community through meeting needs, caring for people, developing relationship bridges, and communicating the gospel in a relevant way.

3. *Source, Not Resource, Giving*

Waldo Werning calls this "supply-side stewardship."[3] This concept involves giving *from* what God has given you, not *to* an institution or organization. What is the problem with a pledge card that challenges you to pledge a certain amount to the church? What is wrong with a pulpit plea encouraging people to give to the budget? What is the danger of a campaign where "All donations will go to the music department"?

The problem with this approach to giving is that unless the leaders carefully communicate that all giving is supposed to be *from* what God has given, it is unbiblical. Instead of giving gratefully back to God, the emphasis is on giving to a maintenance-oriented need. Don't misunderstand: It is important to let people know the specifics of a challenge. That is a part of vision casting. But communication about financial stewardship should be based on the biblical foundation that all giving comes from what God has graciously given. This means opportunities for giving should always begin with what God has provided, not what is needed. It is source, not resource, giving—giving from the Source, not resourcing some project. It is my perception, and biblically supportable, that if the people in your church consistently practice supply-side stewardship, the issue of giving to some project would never surface. There would simply be no need.[4]

I feel fortunate that my wife and I learned and employed this concept early in our marriage. We learned it while I was in seminary. It wasn't through a class but was the result of a talk given by Dr. Bob Grunow. Dr. Grunow taught fundamental Christian financial concepts to young seminary students. His teaching introduced me to a paradigm shift that completely changed my understanding of how God finances mission. Suddenly, our annual income (which wasn't much in those days) was important to know, not just from a tax perspective but from a Kingdom perspective! I suddenly realized that God has given us everything—and allows us to keep the largest portion of it. But from all God gives, we have the privilege of giving a relatively small portion back. Through the years, as our earnings have increased, it is still exciting to focus on giving from what God provides. God also gives us the privilege of deciding where those resources (above and beyond the tithe to our church) should be distributed for the most effective Kingdom impact. As R. G. LeTourneau said, "The question is not how much of my money I give to God, but how much of God's money I keep for myself."[5] Supply-side stewardship is a powerful, biblical concept that promotes a healthy economic environment for enterprise ministry. In fact, without this biblical perspective, I believe enterprise ministries can become a financial crutch for your church. With this principle clearly understood and practiced, your church can thrive as you engage the culture.

4. Vision Casting

I first heard this articulated by Jim Manthei. Jim is a highly visionary Christian who has also been financially blessed by God. He has understood for years that when a vision is cast, it gives those who have learned the first three stewardship principles an opportunity to intelligently and enthusiastically direct their resources to strategic ministries. As you cast a vision for an enterprise ministry at your church, the foundation that should be laid is one of biblical stewardship principles. This includes the principle that vision precedes provision.

Before Jim put this concept in verbal form for me, I recognized this in churches I consulted. When I interview people as a part of the consultation process, I often hear, "the church is always short of money." Most of the people simply categorize it as a "money issue." But that is only the symptom, not the cause. As trained consultants, we are constantly digging for the "issue behind the issue." When churches are repeatedly short of resources, the issues behind the issue are frequently a lack of stewardship teaching coupled with a lack of vision casting.

Casting vision is always the responsibility of leadership. If the leadership doesn't cast vision, no one else will. It is a function of leadership that cannot be delegated. Not long ago I worked with a church in northern Saskatchewan that, among many other challenges, had severe financial difficulties. As the consultation continued, it became clear that the pastor did not have the gift of leadership, nor had he been trained in leadership principles. In addition, the pastor was hesitant to allow the members with the gift of leadership to exercise their leadership within the congregation. This anemic congregation was starved for vision. One of my roles as an interventionist was to pull the vision from the pastor and key leaders and then reflect that vision to the congregation. With full support from the staff and leadership, the congregation rallied around the vision. Guess what? Finances have greatly improved. And why not? Vision precedes provision.

Good biblical vision casting is birthed from the biblical worldview that God is a god of abundance. I call it the abundance principle. Our research shows that many Christians believe the unbiblical idea that God is a god of scarcity, not abundance.[6] This is severely detrimental to the stewardship of a congregation. It cripples individual Christians. It will cripple your attempts to start an enterprise ministry. If you are led by God to start a Jesus enterprise ministry, lay a good foundation about this abundance principle.

Ever been at a meeting where a suggestion for a new ministry was made, but even before the vision was cast, someone asked, "How much will *that* cost?" The first question to ask is, "Is it God's will?" Because if God is in it, God will pay for it. God pays for what is ordered. That is the abundance principle.

The scarcity worldview approaches ministry without seeking God's will. It demonstrates a belief that God can't do everything claimed in Scripture. The God of the Bible, however, owns the "cattle on thousands of hills."[7] God asks people, "Put me to the test and you will see that I will open the windows of heaven and pour out on you in abundance all kinds of good things" (Malachi 3:10). Jesus says, "The Father will give you whatever you ask of him in my name" (John 15:16). The apostle Paul says, "And God is able to give you more than you need, so that you will always have all you need for yourselves and more than enough for every good cause" (2 Corinthians 9:8). Paul understood and practiced the Jesus enterprise way of ministry.

You have to have vision to be farsighted. But, in the church, as my friend Barry Kolb frequently says, "The farsighted tend to get blindsided by the nearsighted!" That's why visionaries are often attacked by those in the church who have no vision. But when the message gets through, and the vision is cast, provision follows. When this, as well as the other stewardship principles, is understood, they provide a healthy balance for enterprise ministries.

5. Right Pocket and Left Pocket Giving

One of my mentors, Lyle Schaller, taught me this concept years ago. He said you have wealth in two pockets. The right pocket is your income stream. It usually shows up in the form of a paycheck. Your left pocket wealth is accumulated wealth. It is wealth that is unearned in a transactional sense but is accumulated through inflation, appreciation, and investment income. It can also come in the form of gifts and inheritance. This, too, is a gift from God. This form of income, once liquidated, provides an opportunity to give a portion (percentage) off the top toward a vision God has provided for effective ministry. What do you think the Kingdom implications would be if every Christian gave from both pockets?[8]

My grandmother never earned a lot of money during her lifetime. But she worked hard and over the years accumulated some wealth. Before she died, she gave ten thousand dollars to my wife and me to help pay down the mortgage on our house. That's an extraordinary amount of money taken off the principal in one payment. Not only that, it also reduced the interest. What a marvelous blessing!

Since we are committed to the biblical stewardship of proportionate giving, my wife and I take 10 percent of all God's financial blessings and give back to God's work through our local church. We also give a percentage back to God's work through ministries we feel are strategically effective for the Great Commission. But, because we also practice left and right pocket giving, we were faced with a dilemma. It was clearly my grandmother's wish that ten thousand dollars go off the principal of our mortgage. But it's God teaching that we take a portion of that and return it to bless God's work. Just because it's left pocket wealth doesn't release us from the responsibility (and privilege) of sharing that for Kingdom purposes. We solved our dilemma by gladly reducing some of the fringe expenses in our lives over the following months, saving one thousand dollars and blessing a ministry that's making a difference. And you know what? We reduced our mortgage, and didn't really miss those "extras" we chose to do without. It was significantly gratifying to be able to invest one thousand dollars in a ministry that would appreciate it.

It would be wise for your church to provide an opportunity for people to donate stock. When investment markets rise significantly, appreciated stock, given as stock rather than cash, provides a significant tax benefit to the donor. This is good stewardship for the donor and a significant blessing to the ministry. Therefore, it is wise for any ministry to have a relationship with a brokerage firm (preferably a Christian broker) who, on the ministry's behalf, can receive stock donations from time to time. The broker then sells the stock, and the money goes to the ministry. I don't advise any church to keep the stock in the market long-term, because the purpose of the church could easily become watching the market instead of making disciples. But, the receiving of stock and the liquidation of those assets provide a good source of income for ministry. This type of donation can be seed money to start up enterprise ministries. It can also give people the opportunity to share their blessings for the purpose of ministry and receive a good stewardship tax benefit as well.

Depending on the economy, investment markets, appreciation of real estate, and so on, there are times when left pocket wealth greatly exceeds right pocket resources. Your church should teach people to think about God's work when they sell land that has appreciated, sell stock that has grown, or receive a gift or inheritance. A portion should first go to God's work. The work of ministry will be greatly enhanced. A Jesus enterprise ministry could be launched.

Your church should also train Christians to put God's work into their wills. This is an excellent testimony to your heirs about your relationship with God and God's work in your life. It also enables you to bless a ministry long after you're gone. When a congregation cultivates both right pocket and left pocket wealth, the whole congregation wins, enterprise ministries included!

6. High-Capacity Giving

Many churches have people of great wealth among their members. Chuck Roome calls them high-capacity Christians for the Kingdom (www.hanfield.org). I worked with a church in St. Paul, Minnesota, where the membership included more than two hundred physicians and one hundred fifty presidents or CEOs of companies. While those titles don't necessarily guarantee financial success, they usually indicate potential financial depth. In my research and analysis of the congregation, I discovered that this church does not offer special counseling for wealthy, high-capacity Christians. Churches often forget that along with the advantages of wealth is the responsibility for effectively sharing that wealth. Bill Hybels poignantly writes, "In almost every church there are people afflicted with affluence. Unfortunately, most leaders don't know how to relate to such people."[9]

Hybels's statement is true of what I see so often in churches. What a shame! It may surprise you, but many wealthy people wonder why the church doesn't give them guidance on how to direct their blessings in a God-pleasing way. Many sincere Christians with significant financial blessing understand the seriousness of what Jesus meant when he said, "Much is required from the person to whom much is given; much more is required from the person to whom much more is given" (Luke 12:48).

As Hybels points out, most pastors are intimidated by high-capacity Christians, or they falsely believe it is "none of their business" to help wealthy people consider how they are to direct their finances. That is not what the Bible implies! Finances are a huge part of your spiritual life.

Billy Graham was once asked, "How much money did multimillionaire John Paul Getty leave behind when he died?" Graham replied, "I know *exactly* how much money he left behind." Everyone was surprised and listened carefully. "All of it!" said Dr. Graham. It is reprehensible that many high-capacity Christians leave this world without making informed, spiritually directed decisions regarding their resources. God's work gets robbed. That is not God's plan for the Jesus enterprise. This sixth principle of powerful financial stewardship involves Christian leaders making sure that those to whom much is given receive special counseling to deal with the responsibility (and privilege) that many of the rest of us will never have.

The Reverend Wayne Hamit from Carrolton, Texas, has developed a ministry called Mountain Movers International (www.mountain-movers.org). It is a counseling ministry for people who have been blessed with financial wealth. Wayne doesn't represent any particular ministry. When he counsels a person, he represents that person. Wayne has developed a unique analytical process to help a person discover his or her unique passion for the variety of ways that God's work can be done. Then he provides ministry options for the potential donor. He helps them examine ministries along the lines of the passion and interests God has given. After the donor selects a ministry, Wayne monitors that ministry to assure that the funding is used accurately and, as a third party, reports to the donor or the donor's heirs (in the event of the donor's death). What an extraordinary idea!

These six stewardship principles are God's financial plan for the Jesus enterprise. They foster an environment for proactive financial effectiveness in any congregation. When taught, understood, and practiced, enterprise ministries develop from a firm foundation of stewardship maturity. This enables a congregation to effectively operate these ministries without jeopardizing the spiritual health of the congregation.

Enterprising Thoughts

- You give as you know and believe, not as you are able.
- If congregations would invest in ongoing training in proportionate giving as a lifestyle, the impact on their financial welfare would amaze them.
- If the people in your church practice supply-side stewardship, the issue of giving to some project would never surface. There would simply be no need.
- The abundance principle: God is a god of abundance, not scarcity.
- Vision precedes provision.
- Churches often forget that along with the advantages of wealth is the responsibility (and privilege) for effectively sharing that wealth.
- The firm foundation for enterprise ministries is the groundwork of solid, biblical stewardship principles. Without them, enterprise ministries can become a financial crutch for your congregation, doing more harm than good.
- The balance of biblical, stewardship, and enterprise ministries provides a powerful dynamic for your congregation to experience God's abundant resources. This enables you to help your community by meeting needs, genuinely care for people, develop relationships, and build bridges for relevant gospel communication. Your church will be healthy, vibrant, and effective.

Next Step Questions

1. Consider the practices of proportionate and firstfruits giving. If this isn't your common giving practice, what is one step you can take right now to move closer toward biblical stewardship?
2. Why is a biblical worldview toward stewardship and financing crucial for a church to be able to effectively

develop enterprise ministries? What unbiblical world-views might you have that you need to consider in the light of biblical truth?

3. Why does "vision precede provision" in a Jesus enterprise? How does that differ from the idea of giving "to the church"?

UNDER CONSTRUCTION: BUILDING IN THE JESUS ENTERPRISE

We shape our buildings: thereafter they shape us.
Winston Churchill

N owhere does the issue of finances become more sensitive than when your congregation begins to focus on the construction of buildings.

Community Church, in a suburb of San Diego, called me to work with them because they were growing and out of room. With the cost of real estate in Southern California, the issue of space has enormous implications. Good decisions are always important.

I quickly learned that the campus had been constructed without a master plan or long-term thinking. One of the critical issues for Community Church was worship space. During the interview process, a majority of the people reflected the purpose statement of their church: "The primary objective is to reach people for Jesus Christ."

To me, the objective outsider, the conclusion was obvious. The sanctuary had to be enlarged and modified to reflect what God was blessing in the church, namely the contemporary worship service. But it quickly became clear that the future of the sanctuary was heading toward a tension-filled standoff. A committee had already been formed to supervise the renovation plans for the sanctuary. Unfortunately, this committee was led (ruled) by a stern traditionalist. His driving motive was far from "How do we accommodate more people so they might encounter the living Jesus Christ?" He was driven by the desire to "showcase our historic traditions." There was a conflict of worldviews: As an outside expert, I supported my client's (the church's) mission statement while the traditionalist leader of the sanctuary renovation committee supported the sixteenth-century Reformation heritage of the church!

This true story represents the powerful influence of the way people think as they approach a building project. How sad that a church prepared to spend millions of dollars and set the ministry tone for generations was hijacked by a committee leader whose primary objective was not in concert with the purpose of the church or the effectiveness of the mission!

Desert Cross Lutheran Church in Tempe, Arizona, also had been growing (www.desertcross.org). This church is led by a pastor who is gifted at equipping and empowering the businessmen and businesswomen in his congregation to take ownership. One of those key leaders was a man named Mike Friend. With a growing number of young families joining the church, and with land and space to build, this church knew expanded facilities were in their future. The big question was, "*But what should we build?*"

After identifying the ways in which God was blessing them and analyzing the felt needs of the people in the community, it became clear that their financial resources should be directed toward a Family Life Center. Mike, who had built a successful plastics company, led the charge to help the leaders clearly identify their best return on investment. The plan would build on the way God was attracting young families to their church. He concurred with my observation that a Family Life Center was the best use of money directed at facilities. The church is now rapidly growing. Why? Not just because they built but because they built right, with people outside the church in mind. Their Family Life Center is a Jesus enterprise.

Here are ten ways you can build effectively. They are valuable for helping you be a good manager of the financial resources God has given you. If you are committed to engaging your culture and developing a Jesus enterprise, they are essential.

1. Clarify Your Objectives

What is your purpose? What is the purpose statement of your church? What did your founding leaders establish this church to be and to do? How does that square up with what you understand the Bible to say about the purpose of your church? How can you be intentional as you develop your objectives? The tendency for most congregations is to think about building in terms of their needs, their comfort, and their interests. But if your mission is directed toward others, then what meets their needs is more important and should be at the forefront of the building strategy.

These objectives are absolutely essential to ponder long before you begin thinking about *what* to build. For most churches, the temptation is to quickly move toward brick-and-mortar thinking long before they have clarified their objectives. It is the leadership's responsibility to squelch that temptation and make sure the purpose is clear.

Bill Wilson has been a key leader of Resource Services Incorporated (RSI), one of the largest and most established ministries that helps churches raise money for capital campaigns. From his years of experience, Bill says one of the most common challenges his stewardship consultants face is a congregation that is eager to build (and begin a capital campaign) but has not thoroughly thought through their purpose and direction. This is where a church consultant can help. I commend Pat Cummins, a long-term pillar of RSI, and Doug Turner, their new president, for developing a system to help churches think through their purpose before rushing into a capital campaign and building project.

2. Learn from Others

We live in an era in Christian history when an increasing number of innovative churches are becoming Jesus enterprises. Their mentality and mission-mindedness is obvious in the buildings they construct. Learn from them. Visit the Ground Level Café at Community Christian Church in Naperville, Illinois. Look at the food court at Willow Creek Community Church in South Barrington, Illinois. Visit the emerging atrium, sports complex, and nine-hole golf course at First Christian Church of Canton, Ohio. Check out the Disneyesque decor of the Sunday school environment of St. James Lutheran Church in Burnsville, Minnesota (www.stjameslc.org). Visit the bookstore at Bellevue Baptist Church in Cordova, Tennessee. Enjoy the performing arts auditorium that allows spectacular pageants at the Grove City Church of the Nazarene in Grove City, Ohio; or the performing arts center at Hillcrest Church in Dallas, Texas; or the one at Faith Lutheran Church in Troy, Michigan (www.faithtroy.org). Study the Family Life Center at Advent Presbyterian Church in Cordova, Tennessee. Work out in the fitness center at Messiah Christian Church in Wells, Maine. Look at the community dental clinic and medical outreach at First Presbyterian Church in Danville, Illinois. Visit the serene campus of the Crystal Cathedral in Garden Grove, California. Don't miss the spacious environment at Southeast Christian Church in Louisville, Kentucky (www.southeastchristian.org). Eat lunch at the New Spirit Café at Marble Collegiate Church in New York City. Stop by the Living Room, a high school and university student hangout in downtown Muncie, sponsored by First Church of God East Central Indiana. Stop by the stellar nursery and innovative children's worship center at the marvelously retrofitted manufacturing plant that has become King of Kings Lutheran Church in Omaha, Nebraska (www.kingofkingsomaha.org). Look at the renovated shopping mall—especially the children's ministry—at Mars Hill Bible Church in Grandville, Michigan. Visit the day care facility, Kid Kountry, at Community Church of Joy in Glendale, Arizona. While you're there, check out the bell tower that is a disguised cellular tower. The list could go on. In my estimation, there are at least five thousand churches in the United States and Canada that have recently built with a driving commitment to a Jesus enterprise mentality. There has to be at least one near you! Find them and learn from them. They will expand your horizons and force you to think innovatively and be open to new ideas. Let God stretch your mind to the possibilities.[1]

3. Have a Mission Focus

The word *mission* means "sent." That means there is a "sentness" about the mentality of what missionaries do. They are always sent *to* people. They are always concerned about speaking *to* the marketplace, communicating *to* the community and engaging the culture. In his Great Commission, Jesus told his followers to "go" (Matthew 28:19-20). He "sent" his disciples out to do mission work (Luke 9:1-9; 10:1-13).

The worldview through which you look at building space should be clearly influenced by a consciousness that your church is a mission center and that your community is a mission field. This is an attitudinal issue, reflected in what the apostle Paul wrote to the Philippians:

> Your life in Christ makes you strong, and his love comforts you. You have fellowship with the Spirit, and you have kindness and compassion for one another. I urge you, then, to make me completely happy by having the same thoughts, sharing the same love, and being one in soul and mind. Don't do anything from selfish ambition or from a cheap desire to boast, but

be humble toward one another, always considering others better than yourselves. And look out for one another's interests,
not just for your own. The attitude you should have is the one
that Christ Jesus had. (Philippians 2:1-5)

4. Focus on Contextualization

One of the primary concepts missionaries learn as core principles of ministry is contextualization: connecting within the context of the mission field. The gospel, in order to be relevant to
the group you are reaching, must be contemporary. Contextualization directs you to be contemporary to today. The challenges of tomorrow will be different than the challenges you face
now. That means speed and flexibility in methodology and style
are crucial. The truth of God, which never changes, needs to be
packaged in a relevant way that presents Jesus Christ as alive
today, which he is!

Contextualization takes into account that your community is
constantly changing. For example, Stutsmanville Chapel, a nondenominational church in the northwest lower peninsula of
Michigan, is a congregation with rural, country roots. The church
is located at a crossroads in Stutsmanville, a little country town
that no longer exists. When I worked with this church, I was bold
enough to say they might consider changing their name since the
town didn't exist anymore. Fortunately, their ministry wasn't as
oblivious to the changes in their area as the name would imply. In
fact, the church was quite adept at reaching new people in the
community. Though the people who founded the church were
blue-collar, rural workers, Stutsmanville Chapel was reaching
upscale businesspeople and those who had taken early retirement
from high positions in major corporations. They were relocating
to what has become one of the most attractive, upscale areas in
the United States. Since the nearby, somewhat exclusive town of
Harbor Springs refuses to allow a fast-food restaurant within the
city limits, I recommended the church move just outside the city
limits to keep the country, northern Michigan feel, but, as part of

its new campus, franchise a fast-food restaurant! They would have the freedom to develop relationships while meeting an obvious felt need in the context of that area.

5. Get Outside Input

Before you spend thousands, perhaps millions of dollars on buildings and before those buildings are conceived as blueprints, get outside input from a church consultant. For a miniscule percentage of the total cost of your investment, you will gain invaluable information to make intelligent decisions and receive objective outside input that will save you thousands of dollars—perhaps more—in mistakes. Use anyone who has the right credentials, has visited hundreds of churches, and has gleaned ideas that can help you.

A church near Denver grew to the point where it needed new facilities. They were going to relocate onto property that was much closer to the highway—a good move for visibility and accessibility. The congregation recruited an architect but was not yet at the blueprint stage of the process. I was called in to look at the early drawings from the perspective of church life, dynamics, and effectiveness. The first thing I noticed was that the parking lot was behind the sanctuary, which hid it from the road. I suggested the drawing be "flip-flopped" so those driving past could see, by the cars, that people were actually attending this church. Furthermore, this would allow for expansion if the congregation were to grow, which was everyone's expectation. I asked the architect if such a rearrangement was any problem and his immediate answer was, "No; that's a marvelous idea!" It was an idea that was probably worth over a million dollars to that church, long-term. The building committee concurred and the plans went forward. Get outside input.

6. Make Sure Form Follows Function

After you clearly focus on your mission and purpose, clearly articulate what it is you want to do. Then determine what facilities you will need to do it. Grace Fellowship Church in New Haven, Indiana, wanted input as to whether they should add an educational building on one end of their facility or expand the office space on the other (www.gfc-fortwayne.org). After clearly analyzing their purpose and objectives, looking at their growth patterns, and making some projections, I led them to a discussion of what it was they really wanted to do. Once that was determined, it was clear to everyone that they should not focus on either one of those projects. Instead, they should relocate. The lead pastor, Chris Norman, gathered the elders. During the elders' meeting, a leader asked, "Well, where should we locate?" Based on the fact that they were clearly a regional church of attraction (due to their distinctive philosophy of ministry), I suggested they locate on a highway where they would be visible and greatly accessible. I suggested they locate somewhere along U.S. 469, the bypass around Ft. Wayne. Another elder said, "How much land do you think we should get?" I replied that, because of the way God was blessing their church, they should look for at least sixty acres— quite a jump from the four-and-a-half acres where they were presently located! Another elder raised the question, "How can we afford that much land on the highway?" I replied they shouldn't sell God short. If it's what God wants done, God will provide a way. Little did I or anyone else know that among those elders was a man who had just sold his company and was praying that God would direct him to where he could invest a large amount of his blessings for the sake of the Kingdom. By the next day, the man had pledged to buy the property. Now the church owns 80 acres and is planning the development of an enterprise ministry campus. Our discussion process benefited the church, and the kingdom of God, in over half a million dollars worth of real estate.

Make sure form follows function. Winston Churchill said, "We shape our buildings: thereafter they shape us." Decide what God is calling you to do. Then determine what you need to do it.

7. Build to Be Practical

While you probably want inviting and contemporary facilities, don't be driven by the need to impress. You are not building a monument. You are not trying to help an architect win an award for a creative building that is utterly impractical for mission. You are, however, trying to make sure your facilities are congruent with your purpose and objectives.

I must admit, for years I both admired the Crystal Cathedral, built under the leadership of Dr. Robert Schuller, and at the same time wondered about its "extravagance." It wasn't until I first spoke at the Robert H. Schuller Institute for Successful Church Leadership that I realized, from the perspective of the speakers' platform, that the Crystal Cathedral is really one of the world's largest television studios. It is built with that end in mind. And rightly so. According to Dr. Schuller, *The Hour of Power*, which is broadcast weekly from the Crystal Cathedral, is a television program seen by more people throughout the world than any other on a consistent basis. That night, sitting with Dr. Schuller at dinner, I confessed my previous ambivalence about the excessiveness of the Crystal Cathedral. I also admitted I finally recognized how very practical the Crystal Cathedral was as a television studio. Then Dr. Schuller added another important comment. He said that some of the most expensive buildings are actually the least expensive. He indicated that if you calculate the cost over the lifetime usefulness of the building, many cheaper buildings end up costing more Kingdom dollars, in the long run, because they don't last. The Crystal Cathedral also engages people in the genre of its Orange County location. Just a short distance from Disneyland, Knott's Berry Farm, Universal Studios, and others, the church has become a significant tourist attraction.[2] Volunteers and paid staff cultivate contacts with a spiritual agenda that, without force, plants the seed of the gospel. The campus of the Crystal Cathedral is expensive. But it is also more functional than most people realize. In a long-term evaluation of per capita impact, it is probably very good stewardship!

I've been in many churches that, in order to save money, built using textured surfaces you would find in a home. Drywall with paint is fine for a private residence, but under the wear and tear of a public building, it quickly becomes dirty, scratched, and unsightly. It's not long before it needs to be replaced. That's when the cheapest construction becomes the most expensive. Upkeep is an expensive responsibility. It's especially expensive when the deterioration destroys a good first impression for new people coming into the church. That's an expense with far-reaching consequences.

There is a huge difference between building a mission center and building a monument. Conduct a careful analysis of what it is you are trying to accomplish. Make sure it is consistent with the vision God has given you. Build to be practical. Build to engage your world.

8. Build Within Your Means

When I was asked to analyze Good Shepherd Lutheran Church near Chicago, it was apparent that the congregation was so financially strapped that its ministry was hamstrung. Every meeting centered around the challenges of paying the bills. But, oddly, Good Shepherd was a growing congregation that appeared healthy in just about every other way. There was no evidence that poor stewardship practices among the people were a contributing factor to the situation. What was at the heart of their financial struggle?

Three years earlier, Good Shepherd had agreed to build a sanctuary that was designed more along the lines of creativity than practicality. While it was quite unique, it became an extremely expensive facility. The congregation didn't have the finances to complete the project, so they borrowed much more than they should have. Worse yet, my growth projection analysis indicated that this new facility would be maximized within a year. Even with multiple services they were still facing sociological strangulation: running out of space and psychologically hindering people (especially guests) from comfortable worship. Consequently, many newcomers, who would have perhaps affiliated with the church, never returned. They went away annoyed because they could not find a seat. The building was too small. The mortgage was too large.

Don't let your mortgage payment become the mission of your church. If you build beyond your means and your ability to pay the mortgage excessively determines what kind of ministry you can do, the mortgage will become your mission, no matter what your mission statement says.

Most churches that build beyond their means cut back in an area that hurts their Kingdom productivity most: staff. Many churches that have built beyond their means are significantly understaffed. This leads to burnout and lack of productivity for the present staff, which leads to less quality ministry. Ultimately, this takes a church from a growth cycle to a plateau and, often, into decline. That creates a scenario in which the mortgage payments become even more severe. I worked with a church in West Virginia that had been crippled by oversized mortgage payments for thirty years. It was a dark cloud that hung over their ministry for three decades!

Whatever you build, make sure you build within your means. That doesn't mean you can't borrow toward a building project. This type of lending is actually an investment in the future. However, when it's all finished, your mortgage payments should be such that they do not become debilitating to the ministry of your church.

One of the ways you can overcome this is by building in phases. Under the leadership of Pastor Tim Huber, Trinity Lutheran Church in Hillsboro, Oregon, maximized its space in an old, worn-out building on a campus that severely lacked parking. They were fortunate to get a spacious parcel of land on a very attractive corner of two major arteries in the area not far from where they were located. We developed a seven to ten year plan together. One of the keys was that they built in phases so that the mortgage did not become the mission.

Each phase was designed to engage the community as a Jesus enterprise. This was implemented from the very first stage. Phase One was the placement of a nice office trailer on the corner of the property with temporary but classy landscaping. The trailer was open during the day and some evenings. The office was operated by volunteers. The sign invited people to enter and explore the future of this parcel of land and the emergence of a different kind of church. Inside the office were brochures, a model, and a videotape presentation that invited people to check out the church at its present location. The office trailer was a small and humble beginning as a first phase. But it was unbelievably effective in attracting people and building excitement. That's why most major upscale housing developments use the same technique!

9. Don't Let Your Ministry Become Building Centered

The average Christian, when you mention the word *church*, will usually think in the context of a building. Yet, Scripture clearly indicates that buildings are only a means to an end and that the church is really a living organism. If your church building were to burn down tomorrow, your church would still exist. Likewise, if your church building was the most expensive and upscale building in the world, but you lost all your people, you would not be a church anymore. The building is just the shell.

Why do so many people think of the church as facilities? One reason is that facilities are a tangible way of understanding who we are. Facilities are a reference point and defining aspect of reality. Good buildings, designed well, tell a story about who meets there and what they do. However, many Christians get hung up on their building because they have been subtly taught for years that the church *is* a building. Either a drawing or a picture of the building appears on much church stationery. Worse, many churches still put a picture of their building on the cover of their bulletin. Every Sunday, people are bombarded with the concept that the church equals the building. Then, when it's time to renovate the building, tear it down, or sell it and move elsewhere, leaders are surprised that people are so protective of that building. The people perceive relocation as a siege on their identity, especially if the present pastor wasn't there when the building was constructed.

One of my favorite church bulletins is from a church in Toledo, Ohio. Grace Community Church designs its bulletin covers with a collage of people's faces. They are caricature drawings of real people who attend Grace. A commercial artist who attends the church takes pictures voluntarily after worship every 3-4 months. The photos are spontaneous pictures of people as they interact during the fellowship hour. Then she draws a caricature of each person and makes them into a collage for the front of the bulletin. In other words, you could worship at that church once and come back the next quarter to find your face on the bulletin! Every quarter, the collage changes, so, sooner or later, nearly everybody gets to be on the cover of the bulletin!

This is an outstanding concept for two reasons. First, you can look at the bulletin cover and immediately see the general age of the people, children's faces, an occasional earring on a man, or a guy with a bass guitar. If you were given a bulletin by a friend, you would have a good indication of whether or not you would feel comfortable at Grace, even if you had never been there. That bulletin makes a great conversation piece when members invite others to their church. Second, it constantly reminds people that the church is not a building. The church is people. During a building program, don't let the ministry become building centered.

10. Hire Your Architect Carefully

The most important aspect in hiring an architect is not what your architect says. It's how willing your architect is to listen. You want to hire an architect who practices ethnology: the discipline of getting inside the hearts and lives of the people you are serving. It is a concept practiced by good missionaries. You want to hire an architect who begins with a clean slate—no preconceived agenda or blueprints.

My friend David Price is an outstanding architect for churches. He describes the role of the architect this way:

> A renowned architect from Canada—Arthur Ericson— defined architecture as the art of listening. He insightfully recognized that good listening was essential to developing competency and skill as an architect. The discussions that regularly occur between architect and client, architect and builder, architect and consultants, and within the architect's own office often require thoughtful review and consideration of the issues at hand. In turn, the architect is often called on to make decisions and provide recommendations. The architect's ability to listen well is essential to responding appropriately and effectively.
>
> While the importance of listening well cannot be overestimated, sometimes what is not said is just as important. This type of listening invites the architect to learn what God is doing with His people. It also engages the architect in a conscious and subconscious dialogue with the land. Every site communicates information about itself: the lay of the land, its orientation to the sun and wind, special features, views and vistas and the overall ecology and history of the property. The architect needs to listen to all of these sources of information with an open mind and heart.

Just because an architect says he or she has worked for numerous churches doesn't mean they understand the unique personality of your church. If they are not willing to listen to and learn about you, then you probably don't want them to be designing your future.

When I worked with Westminster Church PCUSA in Jackson, Tennessee, they were meeting temporarily in a school. They are a new church pastored by a young couple, Brian and Tracie Stewart. These new, energetic pastors have a great heart for engaging the community. They want to develop a Jesus enterprise type of ministry.

They hired an architect who had worked with a number of churches in their denomination. But he was insensitive to the small size of their church and had never worked with an infant congregation with severely limited funds. The members of the church faithfully donated the thousands of dollars required for the architect to create blueprints. In the process, Brian, Tracie, and the leaders carefully told the architect about the financial limitations and restrictions they faced. Despite their communication, this architect designed a facility that wasn't even close to what the church could afford.

Eventually, they were able to hire an architect who was sensitive to the context of their community. He recognized that their facility needed to have a certain appearance but also had to be practical and within their means. They have now built that facility and the congregation is flourishing. Hire your architect very carefully!

Enterprising Thoughts

- Nowhere does the issue of finances become more sensitive than when your congregation begins to focus on the construction of buildings.
- For most churches, the temptation is to quickly move toward brick-and-mortar thinking long before they have clarified their objectives.
- Before you spend thousands, perhaps millions of dollars on buildings and before those buildings are conceived as blueprints, get outside input from a church consultant.
- Don't let your mortgage payment become the mission of your church.
- Many Christians get hung up on their building because they have been subtly taught for years that the church *is* a building.
- Hire your architect very carefully!

Next Step Questions

1. Of the ten ways you can build effectively, which one took you most by surprise? How would an outside consultant be able to help your church build for mission instead of maintenance?
2. Why do you think so many Christians see the church as a building and not as people? How do you think that might hinder effective outreach?
3. How can "the building" become an end in itself? What steps can you take now to ensure that the focus stays on the mission?

CHAPTER TEN

DYNAMIC ENTERPRISE WORSHIP

Between the stained glass windows of corporate
plaster walls of our sanctuaries, our concepts of
and attitudes toward God, ourselves, and others
are being fashioned, for better or for worse.

Sally Morganthaler

Perhaps one of the most visible dimensions of cultural engagement for many Christians has been the contemporization of worship styles. With more people being engaged and coming to Christ through new worship styles, every Christian should be enthused and clamoring for more—right? Wrong. For many churches, contemporary worship services have spawned what some call "worship wars."

The worship service is like the tip of an iceberg. It is the most visible aspect of the community of Christians known as the church. Most of the worship wars, however, are not really about the styles of worship. They are about different postures toward the culture. Remember the different postures described in chapter 1 of this book? The way you understand worship styles (as well as programming, building, dress codes, and such) is reflective of your posture as a Christian.

Several years ago, I had the opportunity to visit a Zulu church near Pretoria, South Africa. For the first part of the four-hour worship service, I noticed the people sang in a very stoic and unengaged manner. Even though the words were in their own language, they didn't seem to be very excited. That surprised me, because I had been to several Zulu villages and had observed these people in their animated and enthusiastic culture. Confused, I asked the missionary next to me, "Why are these people so formal? It doesn't seem like they're very excited. They're singing in their own language, right?" The missionary replied that while the songs were in their language, they were a direct translation of German songs sung in German style and tempo. They had been force-fed to the Zulus more than a hundred years before when German missionaries came to South Africa from Europe. Then the missionary told me to wait a few minutes for the "truly Zulu" part of the worship service.

Soon, the congregation moved into a different kind of music. It was indigenous Zulu worship, within the context of their culture. Immediately, the place exploded! The volume of the singing went up. The people started dancing. The pastor began to do a famous Zulu dance called "hole-stomping," a name indicating that he put his foot down so hard when he danced that it put "a hole in the earth." These people were suddenly alive! They were engaged. I realized it doesn't take a church consultant to know that when the culture's engaged and when worship is in the heart language of the people, Christianity is dynamic. This was the Jesus enterprise at worship!

At Rolling Hills Community Church in Zellwood, Florida, they have decorated their worship space in a way that reflects the environment just north of Orlando. The large cross at the front of the sanctuary is made of living ferns—the same foliage found outside the large glass doors that form the walls of the sanctuary. This, too, is speaking in the heart language and engaging the context of the community. Family of Christ Church in Petoskey, Michigan, has a building built like a log cabin. For that part of northern Michigan, it reflects a cultural expression of that region. Engaging worship reflects the context of the culture of the community.

Providing worship that strengthens the believers but also reaches non-Christians in a relevant way is no small challenge. I call it "stylizing." When it happens well, worship is an encounter for both non-Christians and believers. The task of stylizing worship sensitively has often been a point of strong contention among well-meaning Christians. Walt Kallestad writes,

> It is theologically incorrect to argue that people of faith cannot encounter God in Christ and be richly nurtured in worship that is self-consciously welcoming to those who come either without faith or from the margins of faith. This is neither a "dumbing down" of worship nor a reduction of worship to "people-pleasing" entertainment.... It is worship that welcomes the nonbeliever, along with the believer, into the presence of God.[1]

What Business?

If you were on trial for spreading Christianity, would there be enough evidence to convict you? That would greatly depend on how you understand your "business" as a Christian.

When Jesus was a young boy, his parents found him in the temple after searching frantically all over Jerusalem. It is apparent they were scolding him when he replied, "Did you not know that I must be about My Father's business?" (Luke 2:49 NKJV). What is the "business" of the Father? If John 3:16 is important to you, his business is loving the world so much that he gave his only son, so people who believe in him are able to be with him for all eternity. Likewise, if Jesus is the master of your life, his marching orders are probably important to you: "Go, then, to all peoples everywhere and make them my disciples" (Matthew 28:19). That was Jesus' top priority, and he passed on that priority to people like you and me who want to follow him. Making disciples is a balance between reaching unbelievers so they might experience a relationship with Jesus Christ and helping believers grow in the faith and have an effect on the culture around them. That is the way the Christian movement continues. It is God's primary business for the people he calls the church.

If making disciples is your top priority, it will always affect your posture toward worship in a way that engages culture. The apostle Paul, who had the heart of a missionary, said he would be flexible in whatever style and programming was necessary—the packaging of Christianity—as long as people were being reached for Jesus Christ (1 Corinthians 9:22). In the history of the Christian church, there came a time when Christians were so hung up on style that the church required a midcourse correction. That correction was called the Protestant Reformation. One of the key messages of the Reformation was that God's grace in Jesus Christ was absolutely indispensable. It was a nonnegotiable of Christianity. On the other side of that statement, however, all the packaging issues—like styles of worship—were unimportant. They could change—and must change—for the gospel to get through. For example, some of the Reformation leaders in Germany recognized that the language of their Bible, Latin, made no sense to the people. So they translated the Bible into German. In England it was translated into English. People were actually burned at the stake for translating the Bible into languages people could understand!

Why would the church burn people at the stake for translating Scripture so people could understand it? *Because the church had the wrong posture toward engaging culture.* Has this changed over the last four hundred years? Sadly, the debilitating effects of poor church posture are still quite evident today. People aren't literally being burned at the stake too often anymore. (Being killed for the faith is common, however, among missionaries today.) More often, Christians are being threatened, harassed, insulted, slandered, and sometimes even fired when they attempt to engage the culture through contemporary forms of worship.

One consistent principle with which many Christians struggle is seeing worship from a "mission perspective," not from a "tradition perspective." For instance, I received an email from a woman who wrote the following:

Dear Church Doctor:

I am on the building committee for our church, and we are involved in developing plans for new worship space. We have quite a challenge before us in that we have varying opinions on the proper height of the pews.

Church Doctor, could you tell me what is the proper height of pews today?

I wrote her back:

Dear friend,

Thank you for your question about the proper height of pews. The truth is, most new churches today are identifying new ways to seat people. Contrary to the belief of many Christians, pews are not in the Bible. You know those big cathedrals in Europe? When those people went to worship, they stood during the entire service. There was no seating.

When the Puritans left England and came to America, it wasn't very long before someone said, "Standing all the time in worship is foolish. We ought to put some benches in the church." So they took a couple of barrels, put boards across them and sat on benches. It wasn't very long before someone decided to put a back on those benches. Sometime later, some-one suggested, "Let's pad these things, so we can sleep during the sermon" (at least that's what I think they said). And so you have it: The evolution of the pew.

But today there are no baseball stadiums, performing arts centers, or theaters where the choice of seating is pews. In fact, many different types of seats have been invented that are much more effective and useful for today's approach to seating.

God bless,

The Church Doctor

A few days later, I received a return email from the same woman.

> Dear Church Doctor,
>
> Thank you so much for your input about seating in worship space. You opened our eyes, and we just can't believe we never thought of that.
>
> Church Doctor, can you tell us, what is the proper height for chairs in the sanctuary?

You see, when you focus on the tradition instead of the mission, you've got the wrong posture. You're focusing on preserving your subculture! From a mission perspective, worship is supposed to be engaging.

The challenge for Jesus enterprise churches lies in cultivating worship that breaks through the stained-glass barrier. This barrier is the religiosity that keeps non-Christians from an experience with God. The stained-glass barrier gives unchurched people the idea that worship is foreign, irrelevant, cold, and confusing. That is a long way from the incarnation—Jesus Christ in the flesh, engaging culture.

Christmas is a missed opportunity to engage the culture for many churches. Remarkably, Christmas is the day when we celebrate how God became a human being to meet people on *their* level! Let's look at a Christmas hymn that I have sung since my youth, "Hark! the Herald Angels Sing." It is a beautiful, theologically sound hymn written by Charles Wesley, who lived from 1707 to 1788. The second verse of this song goes like this:

> Christ, by highest heaven adored;
> Christ, the everlasting Lord;
> late in time behold him come,
> offspring of a virgin's womb.
> Veiled in flesh the Godhead see;
> hail th'incarnate Deity,
> pleased with us in flesh to dwell,
> Jesus, our Emmanuel.
> Hark! the herald angels sing,
> "Glory to the newborn King!"

(*The United Methodist Hymnal* [Nashville: The United Methodist Publishing House, 1989], no. 240)

Did I learn this hymn as a child? Yes. Does it rouse in me all sorts of nostalgic emotions from my childhood? Yes. Should in be used in twenty-first-century worship in America? Probably not!

Before you get angry and defensive and consider this to be too radical, answer these questions:

- "Hark! The Herald Angels Sing." What is a herald angel?

- Note the line, "Hail th'incarnate Deity." What does the word *incarnate* mean?

- Note the line that says, "Jesus, our Emmanuel." What does *Emmanuel* mean?

If you know the answer to those three questions, congratulations! You are in a group of one out of five people I interviewed who are seventeen years old and older, who attend church regularly. In other words, 80 percent of the people in worship, many of whom have sung this song for years, might as well be singing in Swahili! Last Christmas I sat in a "contemporary" worship service where we sang, "Gloria, gloria, in excelsis Deo"—in Latin, in the twenty-first century!

What is amazing is that Christmas brings more visitors to worship than practically any other time of the year! So should this song be sung? Probably not—at least not in its present form. Could it be translated so that people could understand its message? Absolutely! The concept of the song and the *meaning* of these words is awesome! It contains a wonderful message that is at the heart of Christmas: God becoming one of us. But if people don't understand it, it doesn't engage them.

Is it not the extreme level of selfishness when Christians perpetuate forms that have no meaning, make no impact, and do not engage, simply because those forms are familiar, comfortable,

easy, and provide fuzzy feelings from the past? Isn't that in conflict with the plea the apostle Paul made to the Philippian
church to consider others more important than themselves?[2]
Worship that does not engage does not reflect a Christian community that is for others, but perpetuates a traditionalism that is
for "members only." It is not just "members only," but members
of long standing, who have been enculturated into the subculture
and have learned to translate archaic expressions into meaning.
When you add up all those preconditions, the number of people
left who experience engaging (incarnate, Emmanuel) worship
are precious few!

Dynamic Equivalence

Communication is always limited by the words used to convey
the idea. My favorite example brings us back, once again, to
Christmas. You have probably heard the song "Away in a
Manger." If so, you may remember the verse that says, "The cattle are lowing, the baby awakes, / but little Lord Jesus, no crying
he makes." Chances are, you have sung this song many times.
Perhaps you have even taught it to your children or grandchil-
dren. The words of this song are the packaging for a great message about the gospel. Here is the question: What does the word
lowing mean? Over the last twenty years, I have found that few
actually know what they are singing.

Lowing is an Old English word that no longer exists in everyday language. It is actually the word *mooing.* The cattle were
mooing and woke up the baby. Now that makes sense!
Christianity is supposed to make sense! When I was young, I
must have been destined to be an analytical church consultant.
Even as a child, I couldn't understand why short cows (lowing)
would wake up Jesus!

In any communication, when the words no longer provide
meaning to the intended hearer, the dynamic equivalence is lost.
That means the original word no longer carries the same meaning. For example, when European explorers traveled to Australia,

they asked the Aborigines what the strange hopping animals were called. The Aborigines replied, "Kangaroo," which, according to one theory, means, "I don't know." But, the Europeans took it to be the name of the animal.

The concept of dynamic equivalence is the approach Bible translators use when they want to reach new cultures with Christianity. For example, if a Bible translator was going to translate Matthew 20:1-16, he or she would have to make a decision about numerous words in that text. There may be a word in the original language of the Bible that has to be translated not only into an English word but also into a word (or words) with the same meaning.

Matthew 20 is the parable Jesus told describing the kingdom of heaven. He says a man hired some workers for his vineyard. Some were hired early in the morning, some were hired later in the day, and some were hired quite late, close to quitting time. He paid them all the same wage and some of the people complained. Those who had worked all day got what they were promised, and those who came in at the end of the day got the same wage. Jesus' point is that people who are Christians all their lives and people who become Christians toward the end of their lives get the same reward.

When a Bible translator puts Matthew 20 into the language of the culture he or she wants to engage, the translator has to make a decision. The original text actually says that the man paid the workers a *denarius*. If the Bible translator wants to be faithful to the words, he or she will translate *denarius*. The problem is that for a twenty-first-century Canadian, Indonesian, Russian, or Brazilian, the word *denarius* means nothing. So a translator committed to dynamic equivalence will translate the word to what it meant at the time Jesus told the story: "a day's wage." Now the parable makes sense. Everybody was promised a day's wage and received it. They got the full payment no matter how long they worked.

Is the Bible translator faithful to the original text? No—not if you are committed to the exact wording. But the translator has the spiritual conviction that God's primary commitment is to the meaning, not the vehicle. So the Bible translator uses the words, "a day's wage." Is the translator faithful to the original text? Yes! This is the approach that virtually all translators use throughout the world. However, when it comes to worship, most leaders, pastors, song leaders, organists, choir directors, and those who publish denominational hymnals fail at dynamic equivalence for the intended audience. This is why so many worship services don't engage the culture they are trying to reach. Unless, of course, the people they are trying to reach are already believers focused more on familiar forms than meaningful truth. But that is not the Jesus enterprise.

One of the most amazing recent movements in Christianity has been the Messianic Jesus Movement (www.cby.org). Recognizing the concept of dynamic equivalence, some realize that many aspects of the Christian faith turn Jews off from hearing about Jesus Christ. But the stumbling blocks for Jews are usually issues of culture, not biblical truth. For example, the word *church* is a Gentile term, not Jewish. The Jewish term for a house of worship is *synagogue*. Jews are used to worshiping on Saturday whereas many Christians choose Sunday. Jewish people call their local leader "Rabbi," while Roman Catholics use the word *priest,* and evangelicals use the term *pastor.* Leaving the Jewish culture behind to receive Jesus as Messiah is an extremely difficult and unnecessary step for Jews. Being sensitive to culture, some reach Jews by asking them to believe in Jesus the Messiah but encourage them to worship in a Messianic synagogue, keep a kosher kitchen, worship on Saturday, and participate in what they would refer to as the Messianic Passover meal. In other words, people in this movement reach Jewish people for Jesus by "packaging" the gospel in culture-friendly concepts. The result? More Jews have converted to faith in Jesus in the last century than in the previous two thousand years! This is not a modern, postmodern, or new teaching. It is the profound issue the early church addressed in Acts 15. It is an approach driven by the desire to engage the culture. It is enterprising worship.

Interactive Worship

The Christian church has historically incorporated interactive worship. For centuries, the liturgical form of worship has had components where the worship leader would say, "The Lord be with you," and the congregation would respond, "And also with you." There may have been a time in history when people actually engaged each other with those words. However, it doesn't happen today, even among Christians. It is unlikely that even the most active and devout Christians stand by the water cooler and say, "The Lord be with you," as a fellow office worker responds, "And also with you." The form may be interactive, but it's not engaging.

In some churches, interactive engagement comes in the form of saying "Good morning" at the beginning of the worship service. In some traditions, it includes verbal responses during the preaching message. This responsive style surprised the man who sat behind the Baptist woman who visited his Lutheran church. A few minutes into the sermon, she said, "Praise the Lord!" A few minutes later she did it again. The third time, the man behind her tapped her on the shoulder and whispered in her ear, "Ma'am, we don't do that at this church!" But then the woman next to him objected, and said, "Yes we do. It's on page 37 of the hymnal!"

One of the controversies has been the emergence of people occasionally applauding at church. Many Christians struggle with this and complain that people who clap in response to a musical piece have a bad theological approach to worship; they are considering church as entertainment. While that may be true for some, it is my perception that this is yet more evidence of the strong need for interaction. It is often seen at weddings, when the officiating minister introduces the bride and groom as husband and wife and everyone in attendance applauds. That never used to happen, especially not in more traditional and liturgical settings. But it's happening more frequently today.

The interactive dimensions of worship are taking many forms. Many modern churches are using visual imagery projected on screens as a part of the interactive engaging experience. It is not uncommon to see screens with the words to songs displayed with a background of moving video. Critics say this practice is negatively influenced by too much MTV. But if the church is concerned about communicating in this culture, one has to ask, "Why do so many people, particularly younger generations, watch, on the average, ten hours of MTV a week?" It is probably because, in this world of highly visual, fast-paced communication, that form is engaging. Forms, in and of themselves, are not good or bad. It is the content of the form that determines value. The form becomes "holy" the instant it carries content reflective of a biblical worldview.

There are many who believe this is an era where the church can recapture the arts. For many centuries, the church was the center for the arts. Some of the best music, drama, painting, and sculpture was centered in the message of Christianity. But over the years, the church lost its presence in the arts and, in some circles, it almost seems as if the church rejected the arts as evil.

Today, in churches committed to engaging culture, there is a movement to recapture the arts and use them as vehicles to share the gospel. Consequently, many churches committed to engaging culture are retooling their worship space from a long, rectangular, classroom style to a fan-shaped, engaging setting, which enhances communication through music, drama, use of video, PowerPoint presentations, and Christian concerts—a performing arts style of sanctuary.

One great way to engage the culture of your community is to involve community leaders in your worship service. Grace Fellowship Church in New Haven, Indiana, was referenced in the previous chapter for their exciting relocation to eighty acres on the highway. There are several reasons this church is growing. One is the engaging worship led by Pastor Chris Norman. Chris frequently invites a leader from the area to be "Community Guest of the Day." On one of the days I was working with this church, Chris acknowledged the principal of Highland Terrace Elementary School. He was not a member of this church but was honored by this congregation in both worship services. The pastor acknowledged the value of teachers and principals and the importance of the elementary school. He also connected it with the free, after-school tutoring the congregation provides in partnership with the elementary school (an enterprise ministry).

Pastor Norman shared appreciation for the work the principal does and asked him to share any prayer requests. Among other issues, he requested prayer for wisdom as he worked with the children, staff, and parents. The pastor then led the congregation in prayer for the principal and his work with the elementary school. This is an excellent way to engage your community on a regular basis.

Here are some people you can honor to successfully engage culture in your community:

- The new sheriff.

- The mayor who just retired.

- The new executive officer leading the community newspaper.

- The high school valedictorian.

- The coach of the high school basketball team whose season just ended.

- The president of the local bank who's just opened a new facility.

- The longtime resident/owner of the local gas station.

The list could go on.

Movement in this direction, like any dimension of Christianity, does not come without risks. Some forecasters have warned, "Watch out for the intrusion of 'churchatainment,'" in which worship becomes "all show and no substance," in an effort to maintain attendance numbers. But it should be understood that this danger occurs not only with contemporary forms of worship but also with traditional forms as well. It is just as likely that a traditional organ concert or cantata can cross the line from ministry to "churchatainment" as any contemporary presentation. In any form, it is the substance—the content—that legitimizes the vehicle as a valuable way to communicate the gospel. In the end, there are only two criteria that determine whether Christian communication in worship is appropriate: substance that is (1) clear and biblical and (2) culturally engaging to the audience you are trying to reach. Without substance, it is entertainment. Without engagement, it is irrelevant.

Charles Trueheart summarized this trend in an article that became widely circulated in the latter part of the 1990s:

> No spires. No crosses. No robes. No clerical collars. No hard pews. No kneelers. No biblical gobbledygook. No prayerly rote. No fire, no brimstone. No pipe organs. No dreary 18th-century hymns. No forced solemnity. No Sunday finery. No collection plates. This list has asterisks and exceptions, but it's meaning is clear. Centuries of European tradition and Christian habit are deliberately being abandoned, clearing the way for new, contemporary forms of worship and belonging. The Next Church, as the independent and entrepreneurial congregations that are adopting these new forms might collectively be called, is drawing lots of people.[3]

There are other ways congregations are engaging people through communication. There are some churches where Christian music is piped throughout the campus to engage worshipers even as they make their way to the sanctuary or auditorium. This would include music in the parking lot and along walkways (like Disney World), in large lobbies (like malls), and in restrooms (like restaurants). There will be an increasing number of churches who obtain low-power radio licenses that cover a couple of miles around the church. Using radio, people can hear announcements and worship music as they drive toward the campus.

First Christian Church of Canton, Ohio, mentioned earlier, has begun a communication trend by hanging television monitors from the ceiling throughout the building (like airports) and airing video infomercials about upcoming events, opportunities for Bible study, and ministry involvement openings. Look for an increasing number of churches that use plasma screens for bulletin boards that are updated by a central computer.

With sensitivity to interactive engagement, I predict there will be an increasing number of worship services where people will be able to "ask the pastor" questions to be answered at the end of the message by using keypads built into the seating. Worshipers will be able to email the pastor at the front of the sanctuary.

Interactive engagement will continue to grow through cybercast activities. Church Web sites will include opportunities for people to give input, visit prayer chat rooms, and watch Web casts of the service. Greg Laurie of Harvest Christian Fellowship in Riverside, California already produces Web casts of worship services. The cybercasts also archive past sermons so they can be retrieved by anyone at any time. Laurie's Web site also includes an online store featuring apparel, books, and tapes.[4]

In order to experience what is new and innovative in worship, attend churches that are on the forefront. These "field trips" will expand the vision for engaging worship for you and other leaders in your church. Also attend a good worship and music conference once every year or two. In my perception, two of the best are "Created to Praise" sponsored by Dave Anderson of Fellowship Ministries in Tempe, Arizona (www.thefellowship.com), and "Break Forth Canada," an annual, phenomenal experience in Edmonton, Alberta, sponsored by Arlen Salte from New Creation Ministries (www.new-creation.net).

Dynamic enterprise worship is not about watering down the truth of the gospel, but presenting it in a way that is relevant to your culture in your day. It's an extremely unselfish thing to do because it may go beyond your own comfort and understanding of what church "feels" like. However, it is nothing less than a sacrifice you are called to make as a follower of Jesus Christ who is determined to be in mission. It is the engaging worship of the Jesus enterprise.

Enterprising Thoughts

- The way you understand worship styles is reflective of your posture as a Christian.

- If making disciples is your top priority, it will always affect your posture toward worship in a way that engages culture.
- The challenge for Jesus enterprise churches lies in cultivating worship that breaks through the stained-glass barrier.
- Worship that does not engage does not reflect a Christian community that is for others, but perpetuates a traditionalism that is for "members only."
- In any communication, when the words no longer provide meaning to the intended hearer, the dynamic equivalence is lost.
- Forms, in and of themselves, are not good or bad. It is the content of the form that determines value. The form becomes 'holy' the instant it carries content reflective of a biblical worldview.
- One great way to engage the culture of your community is to involve community leaders in your worship service.

Next Step Questions

1. Before reading this chapter, had you ever heard the concept of dynamic equivalence? How does a commitment to dynamic equivalence require changes in traditional forms? Read Matthew 20 in the King James Version and in a newer translation. Which translation is the best example of dynamic equivalence for our culture? Which type of translation do you use? Which does your church use?
2. Which is your church more involved in: engaging worship or "churchatainment"? If it is "churchatainment," what are some danger signs that lead you to believe this?
3. List all the ways your church is currently interactive in contemporary ways. What else could be added? How would more interaction engage people in your community who are far from God?

Enterprise Ministries God Is Blessing

There are literally hundreds of enterprise ministries that God is blessing today. Here are a few examples to help make your church one of them.

Perhaps the most common example of an enterprise ministry is the Christian school. Schools present a fabulous opportunity to meet a felt need, especially where parents believe the educational system is flawed to the point where it warrants alternative options. The socioeconomic level of the parents must be high enough to afford whatever tuition costs are established. In some communities, this disqualifies a Christian school as an option unless it is highly subsidized from some other source. One of the best Christian schools I have seen is located at Woodland Presbyterian Church in Memphis, Tennessee. To increase third-source funding, this school has a full-time development director and part-time assistant.[1]

Schools are great enterprise ministries because they provide opportunities for ongoing engagement. If a child enters kindergarten in a Christian elementary school, and the school has eight grades, the ministry has nine years (nearly ten months out of each year), five days a week, to influence the child in a discipling way.

Since parents who enroll their children in Christian schools usually have a high commitment to their child's quality of life, it is likely they will also have high involvement in their child's education and activities. This provides opportunities to engage the parents as well as the child.

The greatest challenge to Christian schools throughout America comes when the staff is not trained in or committed to the purpose of the church (to make disciples), and the enterprise opportunities they must cultivate. This causes both the school and church to operate well below their potential.

As the U.S. (and other nations) has witnessed an influx of people from Mexico, Asia, and other parts of the world, we have seen churches respond to an obvious and important felt need. Since many of these people do not know the common language of their new country, there is an opportunity to teach English as a second language (ESL).

Our Saviour's Lutheran in Sioux City, Iowa, is a church surrounded by many Hispanic people. This old Anglo congregation has literally reinvented itself by adding a Hispanic pastor to the staff. Pastor Ortiz brought a congregation with him, and now there are two congregations within one church: Our Saviour's and El Renacimiento. One of the key enterprise ministries is the ESL program the church provides for people who want to learn English.

It is a known fact that new immigrants to a country are often receptive to new experiences. That means they are not only open to learning English but also open to other new experiences, like the gospel of Jesus Christ. ESL teachers frequently use the Bible as their textbook, so as people learn English, they're learning it from the Bible. ESL isn't just effective in English-speaking countries; many people throughout the world have an earnest desire to learn English because it is a primary trade language. Following Operation Iraqi Freedom, this will likely become increasingly true for Iraqi people and others in Arab nations.

I conducted a seminar in Phnom Penh, Cambodia, soon after the fall of the dictator Pol Pot. The seminar was organized to train the few Christian leaders who survived the massacre of the previous years. While there, I met two women from the United States who were using the Bible to teach English to high school students. The children were from Buddhist homes, but their parents supported their efforts because they saw value in the opportunity to learn English.

Heritage Church in Moultrie, Georgia, has a Hispanic community at its doorstep. Using one of its multipurpose rooms, this predominately Anglo congregation, with help from a new Hispanic pastor, Ed Amezcua, has started a church within a church. In an effort to bring people together from both churches, Heritage has initiated activities like carry-in Mexican meals and weekend soccer festivals. Heritage has engaged its community by embracing its diversity with appealing food choices and a rising sport.

Homeless shelters create excellent opportunities to meet felt needs, demonstrate genuine care, and develop relationships for sharing the gospel in a relevant way. Peace Lutheran Church in Lombard, Illinois, is a congregation that has turned most of its building into a place for homeless people to rest, particularly during the frigid days and nights of winter (www.peacehome.org). Pastor Duane Feldmann explains that the church opens its doors on a rotation basis, along with other churches in the area. The response is outstanding. The staff at Peace interacts with those who come for shelter and food, developing relationships and sharing the good news of Jesus Christ. This enterprise ministry has energized the entire congregation as people experience the joy of sharing love and concern as well as the good news of Jesus with people, many of whom are very discouraged.

One growing enterprise ministry answers the following question: What is the twenty-first-century version of a church potluck? A food court! On a smaller scale, it can be a catered food service. Maranatha Christian Fellowship is an independent church in Lagrange, Indiana. They have partnered with a local food service to serve Sunday lunch in their building. Each Sunday, following worship, the restaurant is available for members. Since it is operated on a nonprofit basis, it provides good food with prices comparable to those of any local restaurant. As a visitor to that church, you receive a guest packet that shares their philosophy of ministry, a daily devotional booklet, and a ticket for lunch at the Maranatha Sunday restaurant—free of charge. Many take advantage of that opportunity, and when they do, they meet friendly members seeking to develop relationships. Even though the second dinner isn't free, many people return to church because of those relationships. The church is reaching out and the congregation is growing.

First Christian Church of Canton, Ohio, has a visitor's center. If you make your way there, a friendly gentleman named John Brakus will invite you to their "neighborhood luncheon" after the third worship service. This is a catered luncheon provided by the food service, which is a full-time enterprise ministry of the congregation. This free lunch isn't just for visitors, but also for staff who circulate among the thirty to fifty visitors who attend this growing church on an average Sunday.

First Church of God East Central Indiana in Muncie is in the process of developing a new campus. They are pursuing a partnership with Burger King in which they will have the freedom to develop an enterprise ministry through a franchise. The new campus will be only a short distance from the area high school, which will create a great opportunity to draw young people into a possible relationship with the church and Christ. That is what might be called a new kind of value meal! First Church also provides a hangout in downtown Muncie called "The Living Room" (mentioned in chapter 9). This provides outreach to high school youth as well as college students from Ball State University.

At First Presbyterian Church in Danville, Illinois, a dentist had a dream to develop a medical and dental clinic for needy people in the area. While the congregation is comprised of primarily wealthy upper- and middle-class people, their surrounding community consists of many who have medical and dental needs but no health insurance. This dentist's desire to engage people led him to start a clinic in the basement of the church. There, he and volunteer doctors, nurses, and other dentists serve the needy people of that community. Those who serve at this clinic have the opportunity to engage the culture around them, showing genuine care and developing relationships. This serves as a platform to share the good news of Jesus Christ. That is an engaging posture in action, and it is bearing fruit for the kingdom of God!

Stutsmanville Chapel is located near Harbor Springs, Michigan (http://my.freeway.net). This church has a reputation throughout the entire region for its poignant funerals. The pastor, a lifelong member of this community, is an excellent preacher, is very personable, and is attuned to the local culture. The church has become a magnet for those who want a meaningful funeral service for their deceased relative, whether or not they are connected to the church. The congregation has developed a quality luncheon ministry following funerals. As I discovered this unique strength through a congregational assessment, and also recognized that the church needed to relocate to obtain more land and become more visible and accessible, I suggested it start the enterprise ministry of a funeral home. Why shouldn't funeral homes and mortuaries be an extension of the church? This is an opportunity to engage people at a very receptive time in their lives. Stutsmanville Chapel has already demonstrated that valuable ministry.

Lord of Life Church, located in Ramsey, Minnesota, is led by Pastor Blair Anderson (www.lol.org). Since 1990, when the church purchased a sixteen-acre property and through additional land purchases, the campus has grown to forty-two acres as it has responded to the needs of its surrounding community. It is a family-oriented and contemporary-styled church.

The sudden accidental death of almost an entire family within the church prompted the leadership to explore what God's vision might be for a cemetery on the property. Lord of Life's first stage of development was the purchase of a monument placed near the entry plaza of the church where the deceased family and others have been buried. Future plans now include a prairie-inspired memorial garden serving the northwest quadrant of the twin cities. At Lord of Life, God took a grievous and painful loss and turned it into an opportunity for a new enterprise ministry.

Sometimes people laugh about the half-truth that banks primarily only loan money to people who don't need it. The truth is that most banks want collateral for their loan. So how do people start when they have nothing? That is an especially important question for immigrants to a new country. To respond to this felt need, several churches have started microloan banks. They are funded by a consortium of donors and lenders who are able to put the right resources together. Microloan banks are managed by Christians skilled in loan management. They provide small loans to help people get started. The loans are often cosigned by a pastor who has supervision of the person taking out the loan. This provides a natural opportunity for a relationship and reaches many people for Jesus Christ while meeting a felt need for an individual and his or her family.

There is no question that, particularly in the U.S., it is a Little League world. Sports play a big part in the lives of families. Bellevue Baptist Church just outside of Memphis has a huge facility surrounded by baseball diamonds and soccer fields. Any family with children involved in sports would be attracted to their Family Life Center by appearance alone! It is one of the largest sports complexes in the entire metropolitan area.

Through a developing partnership, Grace Community United Methodist Church and a local YMCA are brainstorming ways to combine their properties into one contiguous campus with a shared mission: a great park to serve the community as a bridge to the gospel. The YMCA currently runs day camps and sports programs and is planning to build a branch facility on its forty-four-acre property. Grace Community Church is developing its eighteen-acre site to include: the Graceland Children's Center, a Community Theatre, a Youth Clubhouse, and an Adult Ministry and Retreat Center. An exciting Green Ministry is already underway turning woodlands into beautiful gardens and prayer walks—connecting people in the community with the God of creation!

Remember the church library? Today, if it still exists, it is located in some out-of-the-way basement room. It is filled with books from the 1950s and 1960s (or earlier). They are poorly kept and many are obsolete. Why? Because the culture has moved to an Internet world and, with it, an "own it" worldview. This has given rise to companies like Barnes & Noble, who, early on, recognized the need for a relaxing environment in bookstores. Recognizing this trend, some churches around the country are building Christian bookstores as a part of their campuses. These bookstores are spacious and provide room for comfortable chairs and couches. They also serve coffee, tea, and soft drinks.

Community Church is located in Fargo, North Dakota. Over the years, the congregation has become well known for its counseling ministry. The pastor on staff was specifically trained for Christian counseling, but his counseling load became so heavy that he resigned from the position of senior pastor and became the Director of Christian Counseling. With the enthusiastic support of the new senior pastor, the counseling pastor runs a clinic at one end of the church facility. Churches, and other agencies throughout the area, make referrals to the counseling center at Community Church. It is an enterprise ministry that not only provides an income stream but also connects people with the church if they are presently disconnected. It is obviously meeting a felt need in the Fargo area because the pastor is booked with appointments year round.

Church of the Isles, a United Church of Christ church in Indian Rocks Beach, Florida, inherited an old, dilapidated building at the back of its property. After our consulting ministry conducted research in the community to determine felt needs, the church decided to renovate the building into a senior day care center. This is for senior parents of people who work during the day or who need to go shopping but do not want to leave an elderly parent alone at home. It is a great ministry to connect not only with the seniors who use the day care but also their extended families who bring them there.

The use of renovated buildings demonstrates that designing for mission isn't always about creating something that is entirely new. Calvary Chapel in Fort Lauderdale, Florida, focused on ministry growth when it purchased its seventy-five-acre campus property in 1996 (www.calvarychapel.com/fortlauderdale). They formed an enterprise ministry that is their own nonprofit construction firm—Gateway Properties. Calvary Chapel has renovated two industrial buildings with over three hundred thousand square feet into new church facilities. Recently released prisoners were hired and received ministry from those at Gateway. The construction enterprise ministries at Calvary Chapel have also expanded into property maintenance and management services. While by no means their primary mission, those services give them entryways into the lives of people who are served, introduced to Christ, and connected to their church.

In his book, *Halftime*, Bob Buford identifies a large number of people who have made a living but now want to make a difference.[2] These are people who are seeking guidance and direction to help them transition into some sort of career that would have lasting implications. In his book *One Church, Four Generations*, Gary McIntosh has reported several churches that offer career guidance for people experiencing "halftime." He calls them bridge ministries that provide "relationships with unchurched people in the community to help these people ease into the church."[3]

Just about every Friday night Kendallville, Indiana, had a recurring problem. Some of the high school youth would ride up and down Main Street and congregate at the shopping center parking lot. It is called "cruising." It is a social event. But it also became, in the eyes of city hall, a problem. It created noise on residential streets as well as major traffic jams for anyone who wanted to shop in the evening, visit a restaurant, or attend the theater. But most people only saw the problem; they didn't see the felt need. The felt need was that high school students wanted to experience community. To them, cruising was a good way to do it. After numerous failed attempts to correct the situation through legal means, two enterprising college students, Tyler Ward and Nathan Hamlin, got the attention of some of the churches in the area. They formed a group that solicited funds and purchased a salvage yard at the edge of town. They removed all the trash from the premises. Through their collaborative efforts, they turned the salvage yard into a Christian teen nightclub. They called it "The Wreck" (www.thewreck.org). Guess what. Cruising all but disappeared! Finally, there was something for young people to do. This enterprise ministry is not on the campus of a church. This ministry went to the community, and it provides a great mechanism for Christian kids to reach others from their own peer group.

Ever find yourself watching a video with your children and all of a sudden the language or story becomes inappropriate? Wouldn't it be great if you could get videotapes of movies that have been edited for general audiences, no matter what they were originally rated? This already happens! You might call them "airplane safe" edited videos. If you have ever seen a movie on an airplane, no matter how the film was originally rated, it has been edited to become "airplane safe." This could be a great enterprise ministry opportunity for churches. Many families would respond to the opportunity to rent videos from an "airplane safe" video store with videos purchased from the same companies that supply them to the airlines. Not only would this kind of enterprise ministry bring income into a church, it would also allow for interaction, relationship development, opportunities to share the gospel and invitations to church. I don't know of a church that does this yet. Want to be the first?

Many churches around the country provide some form of senior citizen housing. For St. Lorenz Lutheran Church in Frankenmuth, Michigan, this idea has blossomed into a retirement village (www.stlorenz.org). This village includes all forms of independent living, assisted living, and full care services. It attracts retired people from a wide area and extends the ministry of the congregation to people in that stage of life. It is a major enterprise ministry and another opportunity for the church to meet a real need in a society that has an increasing number of people in their retirement years.

Reinventing a main street church is a concept that has captured the imagination of many. It has come into reality at The Life Christian Church in West Orange, New Jersey (www.tlcc.org). The Life Christian Church was first planted in the basement of an existing downtown church located on Main Street. Under the leadership of its pastor, Terry Smith, this "basement church" grew and eventually moved a few blocks away to a storefront, also located just off Main Street, near the town's aging main square. City efforts to economically revitalize the square in the past had brought about few changes. Today, the presence of The Life Christian Church is one of several factors that have resulted in a resurrection of activity. New people are being attracted to the area. New restaurants and stores have followed.

The renewal of the Main Street town square is matched by the spiritual transformation occurring within The Life Christian Church. On the physical side, the church's renovation efforts have included a storefront facelift, attractive building signage, and major interior improvements. Upon entering the new church, members and guests are welcomed at an inviting reception counter that opens onto a concourse lined with park benches and indoor trees accented by tivoli lights. You can hear the voices of children playing in the KidZone. You can smell the aromas from the cappuccino bar, deli, and small food court. The worship space is a multipurpose room with a stage. The worship experience is contemporary, supported by a talent-rich band of singers and performers.

The Life Christian Church has brought the energy and creativity of the city into its space. It is an enterprise ministry engaging Main Street. It is an ethnically diverse congregation, which is also reflected in its leadership. With encouragement from the city, the church has recently acquired a beautiful estate property in the town as part of its growing campus. The social nature of the church with its concourse and cappuccino bar and its commitment to children, families, and performing arts will eventually be transposed entirely to the new campus setting. It will leave behind a rejuvenated Main Street experiencing a new chapter of life.

Vision is always a key to launching an enterprise ministry. Under the leadership of its pastor, Robert Owens, University Family Fellowship in Reno, Nevada, has developed an exciting vision of enterprise ministry (www.uffm.org). University Family Fellowship—the biggest little church in Reno—purchased and successfully zoned its 105-acre property as a "mission field." To do so the church had to successfully complete a land exchange with a county parks and recreation department, annex the property into the city of Reno, amend the regional plan, and secure a Conditional Use Permit and building permits. Enterprise ministries like this require persistence, determination, leadership, and an abundance of faith. In order to penetrate the culture, and build necessary support from the community and the city, the church needed a focus. The vision—also expressed in the campus master plan—helped to make the focus possible.

The new church campus is located within a rapidly developing portion of the city. The property lies on a hillside overlooking downtown Reno. The property also provides an important trailhead entry to Keystone Canyon and Rancho San Rafael Park. The campus main entrance from Keystone Avenue (which connects the site to downtown Reno) and the visual dominance of Keystone Canyon, each provide a unique thematic identity, which may become their name: Keystone Community Church.

This Jesus enterprise is called The Keystone Community Development Corporation. It is overseeing the development of the property. A landscaped backbone road provides access to the campus, which will include a professional office and conference center, senior housing, a community park and recreation center, family life center, memorial gardens, and a performing arts and worship center. Keystone Community Development Corporation intends to develop partnerships with the leaders of the city to bring this vision to fruition.

These are only a few of the many enterprise ministries God is blessing. The rapid growth of coffee and espresso bars, retreat centers, sports camps, and marriage enrichment centers seem to be growing every day. I recently heard of a church in Greenwood, Indiana that has plans to build a climbing wall to attract young athletes in their community.

Wherever there are felt needs, there are opportunities for relevant ministry. Wherever the church has a vision and a commitment to mission, creative ministries will be developed. These ministries will effectively meet needs and demonstrate the integrity of Christian care. This genuine care for people will make it possible to develop relationships with those far from God. These relationships will create a platform that will enable God's people to share the gospel of Jesus Christ in a relevant way. It's called the Jesus enterprise. It's a model given to us by the Lord himself.

And it works!

Enterprising Thought

- Wherever there are felt needs, there are opportunities for relevant ministry.

Next Step Questions

1. Look back through the list of enterprise ministries God is blessing. Which ministries may fit with your location

and culture? What felt needs exist in your area that one of these ministries could meet? How would you make sure you were sharing the gospel in each ministry? Want more ideas of enterprise ministries? Want to add what you are doing? Want to share the story of an enterprise ministry you know about? Log onto www.thejesusenterprise.com and join the movement.

2. How has your perception of your purpose as a Christian, as well as the purpose of your church, changed throughout the course of reading this book?

3. Reread each of the "Enterprising Thoughts" at the end of each chapter. Where can you begin to help your church become a Jesus enterprise?

NOTES

Introduction

1. *Ladies' Home Journal*, August 2001, p. 16. For more information on Brentwood Baptist Church and Messiah Christian Church, see www.brentwoodbaptist.org and www.messiahchristianchurch.org.

2. George G. Hunter III, *Radical Outreach: The Recovery of Apostolic Ministry and Evangelism* (Nashville: Abingdon, 2003), pp. 198-99.

3. Thomas G. Bandy, *Road Runner: The Body in Motion* (Nashville: Abingdon, 2002), p. 59.

4. Tim Wright, *The Prodigal Hugging Church: A Scandalous Approach to Mission for the 21st Century* (Minneapolis: Augsburg Fortress, 2001), p. 20.

5. Warren Webster, in *Theology and Mission: Papers Given at Trinity Consultation, No. 1*, ed. David J. Hesselgrave (Grand Rapids, Mich.: Baker Book House, 1978), p. 261.

6. Leith Anderson, *A Church for the 21st Century* (Minneapolis: Bethany House, 1992), p. 45. See also http://growcenter.org.

1. What's Your Posture?

Epigraph. Tim Wright, *The Prodigal Hugging Church: A Scandalous Approach to Mission for the 21st Century* (Minneapolis: Augsburg Fortress, 2001), p. 12.

1. H. Richard Niebuhr, *Christ and Culture* (New York: Harper and Brothers, 1951).

2. Walt Kallestad, *Turn Your Church Inside Out: Building a Community for Others* (Minneapolis: Augsburg Fortress, 2001), p. 12. See also www.joyonline.org.

3. Wright, *The Prodigal Hugging Church*, p. 12.

4. Charles Van Engen, speech to the American Society for Church Growth, November 19, 1994. See also www.fuller.edu.

5. Kallestad, *Turn Your Church Inside Out*, p. 18.

6. Terry M. Crist, *Learning the Language of Babylon: Changing the World by Engaging the Culture* (Grand Rapids, Mich.: Chosen Books, 2001), p. 34. See also www.citichurch.com.

7. Ibid., p. 49.

8. Ravi Zacharias, "Reaching the Happy Thinking Pagan: How Can We Present the Christian Message to Postmodern People?" *Leadership* 16 (Spring 1995), pp. 18-27. See www.gospelcom.net and www.christianitytoday.com/leaders.

9. Crist, *Learning the Language of Babylon*, p. 16.

2. Influencing Culture by Engaging Culture

Epigraph. Paul Borthwick, "I Am an Ambassador," *Rev. Magazine* (November/December 2001), p. 26. See also www.borthwicks.org.

1. Heard on WAJI-FM, 95.1, October 2, 2001. The pledge of allegiance in rap was performed by the fourth grade class at Indian Village Elementary School in Fort Wayne, Indiana.

2. Tim Wright, *The Prodigal Hugging Church: A Scandalous Approach to Mission for the 21st Century* (Minneapolis: Augsburg Fortress, 2001), p. 11.

3. Rick Warren, *The Purpose-Driven Life: What on Earth Am I Here For?* (Grand Rapids, Mich.: Zondervan, 2002), p. 299. See also www.purposedrivenlife.com.

4. Walt Kallestad, *Turn Your Church Inside Out: Building a Community for Others* (Minneapolis: Augsburg Fortress, 2001), p. 41.

5. Gary L. McIntosh, *One Church, Four Generations: Understanding and Reaching All Ages in Your Church* (Grand Rapids, Mich.: Baker Book House, 2002), pp. 20-21. See also www.mcintoshcgn.com.

6. William Lobdell, "Televangelist Adds Telemarketing to Divine Calling," *Los Angeles Times*, June 3, 2001, sec. B, p. 6.

7. Gary L. McIntosh, *Biblical Church Growth: How You Can Work with God to Build a Faithful Church* (Grand Rapids, Mich.: Baker Books, 2003), p. 123.

3. Enterprising the Audience

Epigraph. Bill Hybels, *Too Busy Not to Pray: Slowing Down to Be with God*, ed. LaVonne Neff (Downers Grove, Ill.: InterVarsity Press, 1988), pp. 93, 164. See also www.willowcreek.org.

1. George Barna and Mark Hatch, *Boiling Point: It Only Takes One*

Degree; Monitoring Cultural Shifts in the 21st Century (Ventura, Calif.: Regal Books, 2001), pp. 168-72. See also www.barna.org.

2. Ray Oldenburg, *The Great Good Place: Cafés, Coffee Shops, Bookstores, Bars, Hair Salons and Other Hangouts at the Heart of a Community*, 3d ed. (New York: Marlowe & Company, 1999), p. 294.

3. Richard Selzer, *Mortal Lessons: Notes on the Art of Surgery* (San Diego: Harcourt, Harvest Books, 1996), p. 46. See also www.albany.edu.

4. Tim Wright, *The Prodigal Hugging Church: A Scandalous Approach to Mission for the 21st Century* (Minneapolis: Augsburg Fortress, 2001), p. 6.

5. Christian A. Schwarz, *The ABC's of Natural Church Development* (St. Charles, Ill.: ChurchSmart Resources, 1998), p. 16. See also www.ncd-international.org.

6. Landa Cope, *Clearly Communicating Christ: Breaking Down Barriers to Effective Communication* (Seattle: YWAM Publishing, 1995), pp. 111-12.

7. John C. Maxwell, "Portrait of a Leader," vol. 2, no. 10 of *Maximum Impact: Direction in Leadership,* Injoy Life Club Audiotapes (Atlanta: INJOY, July 1998), audiocassette. See also www.injoy.com.

4. Culture-Sensitive Communication

1. See Kent R. Hunter, *Move Your Church to Action* (Nashville: Abingdon, 2000).

2. Ibid., pp. 161-74.

3. Mark Conner, *Transforming Your Church: Seven Strategic Shifts to Help You Successfully Navigate the 21st Century* (Kent, England: Sovereign World, 2000), p. 70.

4. Terry M. Crist, *Learning the Language of Babylon: Changing the World by Engaging the Culture* (Grand Rapids, Mich.: Chosen Books, 2001), p. 99.

5. George Hunter III, Dean of the School of World Missions/Evangelism, Asbury Theological Seminary, speech to the American Society for Church Growth, November 1997.

6. Alison Stein Wellner, "O Come, All Ye Faithful: Religious Institutions Attempt Marketing Miracles to Bring Young Adults into the Fold," *American Demographics* (June 2001), pp. 51-55. See also www.marblechurch.org.

7. Ibid., p. 54. See also www.hillcrestchurch.org.

8. Leonard Sweet, *Post-Modern Pilgrims: First Century Passion for the*

21st Century World (Nashville: Broadman and Holman, 2000), pp. 112-13. See also www.leonardsweet.com.

9. Crist, *Learning the Language of Babylon*, p. 105.

10. Michael Fullan, *Leading in a Culture of Change* (San Francisco: Jossey-Bass, 2001), p. 5. See also www.michael fullan.com.

11. Rick Warren, *The Purpose-Driven Church: Growth Without Compromising Your Message & Mission* (Grand Rapids, Mich.: Zondervan, 1995), p. 228.

12. Kent R. Hunter, *One-On-One Witness* (Corunna, Ind.: Church Growth Center, 2001), audiocassette.

13. Don Peppers and Martha Rogers, *The One to One Future: Building Relationships One Customer at a Time* (New York: Doubleday, 1996), pp. 26-27, 261-62. See also www.1to1.com.

14. Lynne Hybels and Bill Hybels, *Rediscovering Church: The Story and Vision of Willow Creek Community Church* (Grand Rapids, Mich.: Zondervan, 1995), p. 164.

15. Tim Wright, *The Prodigal Hugging Church: A Scandalous Approach to Mission for the 21st Century* (Minneapolis: Augsburg Fortress, 2001), p. 14.

16. David S. Luecke, *Apostolic Style and Lutheran Substance: Ten Years of Controversy over What Can Change* (Lima, Ohio: Fairway Press, 1999), pp. 25-31.

17. Elmer L. Towns and Neil T. Anderson, *Rivers of Revival* (Ventura, Calif.: Regal Books, 1997), p. 98. See also www.ficm.org and www.elmertowns.com.

5. Leadership for Enterprise Ministries

Epigraph. John C. Maxwell, *The 21 Irrefutable Laws of Leadership: Follow Them and People Will Follow You* (Nashville: Thomas Nelson, 1998), p. 42.

1. Kent R. Hunter, *Activating Members for Ministry* (Corunna, Ind.: Church Growth Center, 1996), audiocassette.

2. Kent R. Hunter, *Your Church Has Personality: Find Your Focus, Maximize Your Mission* (Corunna, Ind.: Church Growth Center, 1997), pp. 105-7.

3. George Grant, *The Micah Mandate* (Chicago: Moody Press, 1995), p. 32.

4. John C. Maxwell, "Portrait of a Leader," vol. 2, no. 10 of

Maximum Impact: Direction in Leadership (Atlanta: INJOY, July 1998), audiocassette.

5. Ibid.

6. Douglas Alan Walrath, *Leading Churches Through Change* (Nashville: Abingdon, 1979), pp. 121-24.

7. The Church Vitality Profile is a product and service of Church Doctor Ministries. See www.churchdoctor.org.

8. Kenneth Blanchard and Spencer Johnson, *The One Minute Manager* (New York: Berkley Books, 1981), p. 39. See also www .blanchardtraining.com.

9. David L. Hocking, *Be a Leader People Follow* (Glendale, Calif.: Regal, 1979), pp. 32-42.

6. Leading the Enterprise Transition Through Positive Change

Epigraph. Henry Blackaby and Richard Blackaby, *Spiritual Leadership: Moving People on to God's Agenda* (Nashville: Broadman and Holman, 2001), p. 23. See also www.henryblackaby.com.

1. See Lyle E. Schaller, *The Interventionist* (Nashville: Abingdon, 1997).

2. Kent R. Hunter, *Discover Your Windows: Lining Up with God's Vision* (Nashville: Abingdon, 2002), pp. 56-57.

3. Douglas Alan Walrath, *Leading Churches Through Change* (Nashville: Abingdon, 1979), pp. 121-24.

4. Michael Slaughter, *Spiritual Entrepreneurs: 6 Principles for Risking Renewal,* Innovators in Ministry, ed. Herb Miller (Nashville: Abingdon, 1995), pp. 134, 136. See also www.ginghamsburg.com.

7. Selling Out? Moneychangers in the Temple

Epigraph. David Shibley, *Challenging Quotes for World Changers: God's Little Book on the Great Commission* (Green Forest, Ark.: New Leaf Press, 1995), p. 107. See also www.jackhayford.com.

1. In the February/March 2002 issue of *NRB,* the organization's magazine, the new and "controversial" president and Chief Operating Officer of the National Religious Broadcasters, Wayne Pederson, approached this subject with amazing clarity and fresh vision that this observer had not seen previously. In his short article entitled "Strategic

Initiative #1: To Make an Impact on the Church and Culture" he wrote about the strategic goals being presented to the NRB Board of Directors. He indicated that his number one vision for the NRB was, "That NRB would lead Christian media to make a strong spiritual impact on the church and culture." He continued by saying, "We can't just talk to the already convinced. We need to impact our culture and the world." He closed his excellent vision statement by saying, "The final indicator of the success of Christian media is not dollars raised, Arbitron ratings, awards, stock prices or headlines. The thing God holds us accountable for is the use of the electronic media resources He's given us to make an impact on his church and our culture. Jesus, our leader, has given us the mandate. That's no. 1 for me—and for NRB" (Manassas, Va.: National Religious Broadcaster, February/March 2002, page 6). Unfortunately, not everyone shared his vision and his procedure for casting it. Wayne Pederson was removed from his position just a few weeks later.

2. Jim Cymbala, *Fresh Wind, Fresh Fire: What Happens When God's Spirit Invades the Heart of His People* (Grand Rapids, Mich.: Zondervan, 1997), p. 69. See also www.brooklyntabernacle.com.

3. Dr. William Bennett is an attorney and an ordained pastor. He specializes in the area of tax law as it relates to enterprise ministries. Bennett says that when a church invites the community to a spaghetti dinner event "to make money for the church," it is illegal by IRS standards (in the U.S.) because it is not in concert with the church's mission statement. How ironic that the legal system of a secularized nation holds the church accountable to stay true to its mission! You can learn from Dr. Bennett by visiting him at www.thechurchcounsel.com.

4. Walt Kallestad, *Turn Your Church Inside Out: Building a Community for Others* (Minneapolis: Augsburg Fortress, 2001), pp. 139-40.

8. Show Me the Money!

Epigraph. Waldo J. Werning, *Christian Stewards: Confronted and Committed* (St. Louis: Concordia, 1982), p. 1. See also www.churchstewardship.com.

1. Ibid., p. 168.

2. Kent R. Hunter, *Discover Your Windows: Lining Up with God's Vision* (Nashville: Abingdon, 2002), p. 65.

3. Waldo Werning has also written an excellent book that takes a deeper look at firstfruits giving, called *Supply-Side Stewardship: A Call to Biblical Priorities* (St. Louis: Concordia, 1986).

4. The Israelites' offering back to God for the construction of the Tabernacle in Exodus 35:20-29; 36:2-7 is a good example of this. Eventually the Israelites gave so much, Moses had to command them to stop. What if *that* happened in your church?

5. *Mover of Men and Mountains: The Autobiography of R. G. LeTourneau* (Upper Saddle River, N.J.: Prentice-Hall, 1991), pp. 279-80. See also www.letu.edu.

6. Hunter, *Discover Your Windows*, pp. 74-78.

7. Psalm 50:10; a biblical way of saying God owns it all and you can't even count it.

8. See also Lyle E. Schaller, *The New Context for Ministry: Competing for the Charitable Dollar* (Nashville: Abingdon, 2002), pp. 185-86.

9. Bill Hybels, *Courageous Leadership* (Grand Rapids, Mich.: Zondervan, 2002), p. 109.

9. Under Construction: Building in the Jesus Enterprise

1. If your church has an enterprise ministry, log on to www.the jesusenterprise.com and share, in a short paragraph, what it is, the name of your church, and its location. If you are looking for a Jesus enterprise church, log on and review the growing list. If you do not find one in your area, check back in a few weeks. The list will grow!

2. Not long ago, I was in O'Hare International Airport waiting to board a flight to Orange County, California. Posted near the gate was an electronic sign that showed the Orange County destination, time of departure, and flight number. The artwork on this sign displayed Orange County attractions. It didn't depict Disneyland or Knott's Berry Farm, but the Crystal Cathedral! That is an engaging enterprise ministry with influence!

10. Dynamic Enterprise Worship

Epigraph. Sally Morganthaler, *Worship Evangelism: Inviting Unbelievers into the Presence of God* (Grand Rapids: Zondervan, 1995), p. 29.

1. Walt Kallestad, *Turn Your Church Inside Out: Building a Community for Others* (Minneapolis: Augsburg Fortress, 2001), p. 75.

2. Philippians 2:3-4 (discussed in chapter 9).

3. Charles Trueheart, "Welcome to the Next Church," *Atlantic Monthly* 278, no. 2 (August 1996): p. 37.

4. You can engage Greg Laurie at www.harvest.org.

Afterword: Enterprise Ministries God Is Blessing

1. This is an example of a good school. Note that the church/school enterprise relationship is fair, but not exemplary.

2. Bob Buford, *Halftime: Changing Your Game Plan from Success to Significance* (Grand Rapids, Mich.: Zondervan, 1994).

3. Gary L. McIntosh, *One Church, Four Generations: Understanding and Reaching All Ages in Your Church* (Grand Rapids, Mich.: Baker Book House, 2002), pp. 110-11.

Scripture Index